How to Hike the Appalachian Trail

A Comprehensive Guide to Plan and Prepare for a Successful Thru-Hike

CHRIS CAGE

www.greenbelly.co

How to Hike the Appalachian Trail
*A Comprehensive Guide to Plan and Prepare
for a Successful Thru-Hike*

This book is dedicated to everyone pursuing the life they want to live.

Contents

Hey, I'm Chris

I joined Boy Scouts much later than most. I was 14, a freshman in high school, determined to get my Eagle Scout. Our troop drove to Amicalola Falls, Georgia for one of my first overnight outings. We hiked a few miles into the woods on a small trail, no more than a foot wide. Bugs, sweat and physical exertion with a bunch of 11 year olds was not my idea of a fun weekend.

While cooking dinner that night, our scoutmaster explained that we were at the very beginning of The Appalachian Trail. This trail continued all the way up the Appalachian Mountain Range to Maine. I can remember looking down that trail, through the small corridor of thick trees, being fascinated that this tiny path went on for over 2,000 more miles.

January 2012, I was 23 and just out of college. Life was good. My accounting major had helped me secure a stable job with a promising career at a large corporation in Birmingham, Alabama.

However, the idea of waking up in 40 years still working

as an accountant was a little terrifying. I didn't want the life where "adventure" was a weeklong trip to Paris with a selfie at the Eiffel Tower.

The real wakeup call came when I noticed my peers doing two things:

1) Getting married and
2) Buying houses with 30 year mortgages.

I knew I wasn't ready for marriage. And, to me, a 30 year mortgage really meant "you need to have a job for the next 30 years".

I felt like the time for freedom and exploration was upon me. I started saving my money and planning my exit. I was going to hike the Appalachian Trail ("AT") - a childhood dream.

Beyond getting my Eagle Scout, my backpacking experience was really only weekend trips with some college buddies. I knew the AT would be a challenging beast and potentially too difficult for me to finish.

Ultimately, I feared failure. I was scared of telling all of my friends and family that I was planning for months to attempt this big epic hike… and then not complete it. I decided I wanted to know all potential areas for failure and prepare accordingly.

The research began. I totally geeked out. YouTube videos, books, spreadsheets, emailing anyone that knew anything, you name it. It was overwhelming and I had a thousand questions.

How much should my pack weigh?
Where will I find drinking water?
Where should I sleep?
What kind of boots should I wear?
How much does it cost?
Is it dangerous?
Should I be doing any physical training?

Despite being overwhelmed, I started to learn more and anticipate how exciting this journey would be.

There is a scene in the movie, *Into the Wild*, where the main character cuts up his credit cards and burns his money. He is eliminating any attachment he has to society before setting off into the uncharted Alaskan Wilderness.

That sense of pure freedom and slight madness is exactly how I felt while planning my hike. Until then, it was as if I had been operating within some sort of boundaries and rules. My life had been on a predictable path. This hike felt like I was going to play hooky... except for 6 months.

In addition to the Appalachian Trail, I started planning a bicycle tour of New Zealand and a backpacking trip through Asia. In New Zealand, similar to the AT, I would either hike or bicycle everywhere. Motorized vehicles would only be allowed when hitchhiking. I really just wanted to 'get out there'.

Several months later, I put in my final notice at work. Dad felt like I was throwing my life away and didn't speak with me for months. Mom cried.

I would not stay in one place for more than a few weeks

for the next 2 years. My bed, desk, TV, everything went up for sale on Craigslist. I moved any last belongings (mainly extra clothes) back into my parents' house.

My gear was ready. Quality items built for a beating. They were also super light. My new tent was so thin; I actually called the manufacturer to make sure I wasn't missing anything. There had obviously been some technological advancements in the industry since my last gear purchases over ten years earlier. In order to reduce pack weight, I shaved off the handle of my toothbrush and cut every extra little bag strap and zipper. Bare essentials only.

I was a Southbounder and, therefore, needed to begin my hike at the Northern terminus at Mt. Katahdin, ME. As I was on a bus from the Portland airport to a hostel near the trailhead, I met a fellow hiker. She had already hiked the southern half of the Trail and was 'flip-flopping' to finish the northern half.

The next morning, we were packing our bags to head out on the Trail. This was the moment I had been waiting for. As I slipped on my pack to hop on the shuttle and head to the trailhead, I noticed she was loading all of her gear into a huge trash bag that was lining the inside of her pack.

I asked what she was doing. She laughed and asked "you really don't have one?" My heart stopped. I was already anxious enough from the pre-hike anticipation. Did I really miss something though?

Apparently this trash compactor bag would be much better at preventing water from seeping into my pack than the pack cover I had bought. Even after all my research, I was realizing before even setting foot on the Trail that I had missed something. She handed me a spare trash compactor bag. It kept my gear waterproof for the entire journey and was clearly better than my pack cover.

Over the next six months, I picked up a lot more tips and tricks that I did not find in books or blogs. And on the cold afternoon of December 17th, 2013, I collapsed on top of Springer Mountain, GA.

Beyond gear, there were countless things that I wish I could have told myself. Things about the wildlife, the logistics and the REAL struggles I would encounter.

People love to talk about how hard the AT is and how miserable parts of it can be. Yes, that is somewhat true. But, come on. It is 6 months! Plenty of miserable stuff has probably happened in the last 6 months of your life, no? There has probably been some amazing stuff too, right?

The AT experience is no different, only on a bigger and more extreme spectrum. At the end of the day, the aches and pains will be trumped by the epic landscapes, great friendships and proud lifelong memories you will have.

The AT is often referred to as a microcosm of life. It has a beginning and an end. You start off with a fearful learning curve, slowly become comfortable and then embrace it wholeheartedly before it comes a finish line. The fearful part is only in the beginning. Once you find your groove, you'll just enjoy the ride (or hike?).

This book is designed to help you get through that first learning curve and planning stage. I want the AT to feel a lot less intimidating after reading this. If I can do it, you can too. Comprende? It really just comes down to a little preparation and mental fortitude.

There were countless times before leaving that I thought "Hmm, this seems really stupid Chris. You are quitting your job to go do something you may not enjoy... and may not be able to do. Maybe this isn't such a good idea."

I am so happy that I made the necessary sacrifices to pursue it. If I could talk to my 23 year old self again, I would scream in my face "This is one the best decisions you will ever make! Don't second guess it. You will be an old man one day and regret NOT doing this more than you ever would doing it."

On a more personal note, the AT made a profound impact on my life. There is something about life that has always felt too fast to me... like it is passing me by and I can't keep up. Pursuing a thru-hike of the Appalachian Trail felt like I was grabbing life by the balls and saying "you are not going anywhere without me!"

Cheesy? Maybe. But, it was one of the best times of my life and that's all that matters. And, for the record, it did feel like I was grabbing life by the balls.

Okay, enough pep talk.

CHAPTER 1

Favorite Tales

Mile One.

The first five miles flew by as I approached the top of Mt. Katahdin on the first day. At 5,000 feet above sea level, looking south at the horizon, I could barely make out the faint trees. They looked *really* far. Those trees were probably only a three day hike away. Even if I averaged 15 miles a day, GA lay 5 months beyond them. Intimidating to say the least.

I had run a marathon a few months prior and felt like I was in pretty good shape. But, I had heard estimates that only 10-25% of thru-hikers complete the Trail. As I sat on top of the mountain, I found out a man had turned around before making it to the top. My odds of being in that top 10-25% were already increasing.

Since I was feeling good, I decided to push on 15 more miles. That ended up being a 20 mile first day… including one of the biggest climbs on the whole Trail.

My legs felt like lead the next morning. They were shockingly sore. I had gotten cocky and was paying the price. I was at the beginning of the 100 Mile Wilderness and knew it could be another week before reaching the first trail town to rest in, Monson, Maine.

I limped along the second day until reaching a shelter (Rainbow Stream Lean-to) that evening. There was a bone-shakingly cold stream nearby. Perfect. I stripped down and rested my throbbing legs in it hoping to numb the pain and minimize any swelling. I met my first crew of hikers that night. They were super helpful. One of them was an army medic and helped wrap up my swelling knees.

The Trail was beautiful and the guys I had met were great. My legs were stressing me out though. I was limping along everyday through the Wilderness and began relying heavily on sturdy branches as crutches. I had read that trekking poles were not necessary. Therefore, I did not bring any. After several days of increased swelling, I nearly crawled into Monson.

I rested there in ice-baths and swallowed a life-long supply of anti-inflammatory pills. On top of the pain, my feet had taken a serious blister beating. I needed sock liners to help reduce the friction.

The hike was off to a rough start and the likelihood of completion was not promising. I talked to a few friends back home on the phone about my injury and began doubting my ability to continue.

After resting for two days, my recently adopted hiking

crew pressed on without me. The third day, I hobbled down to the restaurant to see what new hikers might be in town. I noticed one of my buddies leaned back in a chair. Why hadn't he pressed on? He had a cast covering his mid shin all the way up to his crotch. Apparently, he had twisted and torn up his knee at a slippery river crossing.

Ouch.

He told me several other hikers never made it out of the Wilderness. They had found rides on some of the logging roads and quit a few days back. Whoa. My hobbled knees had made it farther than those guys?

As I felt the tiniest smidge of confidence, my knees started to feel better.

After 5 days of resting, the swelling had gone down. I also purchased sock liners and trekking poles. There were some new hikers in town and I was ready to hike out.

In hindsight, that first week was probably my toughest. I feared the unknown and didn't need to.

Simple Life.

After about a month of hiking, the Trail and, the woods in general, began to feel more like a home and less like an obstacle.

I specifically remember walking along a grassy ridge in Vermont one morning. The trail was narrow and the grass was thick. The grass was covered in heavy dew and, as my shoes brushed alongside the blades, my feet and socks slowly began to get wet. I groaned in annoyance. My feet would be steamy all day and had the potential to form blisters by the time I reached the shelter.

Ugggghhhh.

The grass became tall, eventually chest high. Walking through this was almost like walking through a football practice tackling machine - pushing through thick grass blades on each side of my shoulders. Now, my whole body was getting soaked. I stopped, groaned again and started cursing.

The thick grass stretched on for as long as I could see. It quickly became apparent how unavoidable getting wet really was. There was no point in fighting it - getting wet was simply out of my control. I could control, however, not being a big fat baby. I was well on my way to a miserable day of hiking for no good reason.

Time to embrace the discomfort.

I stretched my arms out and grazed the tops of the grass blades allowing as much surface area of my body to make contact with the dewy grass. With each step, the dew droplets quickly accumulated and fully drenched everything. It felt great to just let go.

Scientists often refer to this as the "Screw it point".

A few days later, my hiking buddy stepped into a muddy hole just in front of me. His foot sank nearly a foot into the goo. He turned around, looked at me and said "hell yea, check that out!"

It felt like I started to embrace the daily annoyances.
Before, I had been logging miles and primarily focused on
the destination. Other than playing in the dirt as a kid,
there were few times in my life that I had practically
welcomed discomfort quite like I did on the Trail. I mean
welcomed it. Like singing-in-the-rain type of welcoming.

For most people, rain means an umbrella... and mud
means a bath... and body odor means deodorant... and a
mosquito means bug spray... and a cut means a band
aid... and hot weather means air conditioning. Most of
those remedies are not an option on the Trail which
became, to me, one of my favorite things. At times, it felt
good to be dirty and not constantly fighting the elements.
It felt natural to embrace it.

Trail Magic.

I was 750 miles in when I had to pull off trail for two and a
half weeks for a family event. By the time I returned, all
my comrades had hiked on and were three hundred miles
ahead.

Okay, this sucks. But, certainly there are some other
Southbounders back here to hike with, right?

The most recent hiker entry in the log book was a couple
days ago. The last real southbound group must have been
at least 40 miles ahead of me. Better than nothing. If I
averaged 5 more miles than them per day, then I could
catch up in 8 days. That meant I needed to put in some big

miles before I could have any sort of social life again.

The solitude began. Several days without so much as vibrating my vocal chords. Well, at least not directed at another human. I was tired. Pushing long days without any social presence was depressing.

About 5:30 PM on a Friday afternoon, I stopped at a gas station near a road crossing. I sat outside on the concrete curb and drenched my head with their car wash hose. I sat back against the wall of the gas station and closed my eyes eating a bag of Cheetos and a honey bun. It felt so good to rest and chomp down on a mound of junk food.

A middle aged man walked by me to go inside and asked if I was okay. After all, I probably looked disgusting. I thanked him and told him yes. We talked for a minute and I told him I was thru-hiking the AT. Without hesitation, he offered me a room to stay at his lodge. Apparently, he had organized a short hike for a small hiking group that weekend. He asked, in exchange for a bed and breakfast, would I mind speaking to his group that night.

I hesitated. I wanted to continue hiking and catch up with the group. It was obvious though - I was tired, lonely and a mess. I agreed to join him.

We hopped in his car and drove a few miles to the lodge. It was actually a spiritual retreat center. He put me up in my own room with cotton sheets and a hot shower. He invited me to a quick, but yummy buffet dinner downstairs.

Eleven of us sat in a circle of couches and talked about

hiking. Some were beginners that just enjoyed stepping outside into the woods, others shared stories of international mountain escapades. I talked about my thru-hike and the events leading up to it.

Afterward, Skip, the man who had befriended me just a few hours ago at the gas station, gave a presentation to all of us on the Hudson River School. It was an art movement in the 1800's focused on the area we were in, the Hudson River Valley and surrounding mountain ranges. He went on about how the land influenced the art and how the art influenced the culture. The discussion quickly turned from Thomas Cole into John Muir and finally Ralph Waldo Emerson and Henry David Thoreau.

Someone else offered to close with a meditation prayer.

The next day, Skip offered to 'slack pack' me. Meaning I left my heavy gear at the lodge and hiked with only some water and snacks throughout the day before he picked me up again 20 miles down the trail. He offered for me to stay another night at the lodge. Free of charge, of course.

With the shower, quality rest, hearty food, fun experience, new conversations and slack pack, I was rejuvenated. I caught up to the Southbound bubble a few days later in much better shape, and probably faster, than I would have if I kept hiking that afternoon at the gas station.

This was one of the most humbling experiences I had on the Trail. Without any hesitation or expectation of something in return, a stranger had been so generous and accommodating. This type of generosity is called 'Trail Magic' and is given by 'Trail Angels'.

I had met some interesting people, learned about the history of the surrounding area and hopped into a group meditation. Not bad for a new and unique experience.

Don't be afraid to say 'yes' every now and then.

Bears.

Having little contact with society, thru-hiker conversations often revolve around the trail experience - wildlife being a common topic. Many had seen moose and bobcats and I enviously listened to their tales. Rattlesnakes had been my favorite sighting. I really wanted a good black bear sighting though. Black bears are notoriously elusive and timid. I had only seen flashes of them through the trees.

My hiking buddies and I hitched out of Front Royal, VA back to the trailhead with clean clothes and full stomachs ready to enter the famous Shenandoah section of the Trail. It was glorious. The bright reds and oranges of fall painted the landscape.

The crowds were nonexistent as well. In 2013, Congress had failed to agree on a budget which, subsequently, caused a government shutdown. Part of this meant shutting down the entire National Park system... including Shenandoah. No one was allowed in, not even thru-hikers. After 3 months of relentless hiking, I couldn't skip a big chunk of the Trail. The other option was to wait for an unknown amount of time for Congress to settle the budget. I mean, what would you do?

We decided to split up and go into stealth mode. I hiked

mostly at night and would "bush dive" from park rangers in the day. I can remember hiking on a desolate Skyline Drive with a clear view of the Milky Way above.

The sun was starting to rise after one long night of hiking. I still had several miles to hike in order to stay on schedule and meet my friends at a shelter the next day. I took a step toward a tree to use the public facilities (aka 'pee'). Just as I stepped forward, a branch above me made a slight crackle. Not wanting to get crushed by the falling limb, I scurried out of the way.

The sound was not a falling limb. It was a black bear sliding down the tree, digging his claws into the tree to brace his descent. He was tiny. Maybe 150 lbs. and terrified that I was near his tree. He thudded to the ground just a few feet away from me and scurried off into the deep brush. Like dominoes, another one thudded down a nearby tree... and another. The bears had climbed up there to sleep and I was the first thing to wake them up.

Over the next few hours, I saw 15 black bears slide down from their perches. One mom with her two cubs crossed the Trail less than 20 feet in front me. She stopped mid stride and just stared at me.

That morning was one of my favorite periods of time on the entire 6 month hike. Not to mention, I certainly got my black bear sighting.

Snow.

My hiking crew and I had only seen small bits of snow

and ice on the Trail in Virginia. By the time we headed south and crossed into Tennessee on November 18th, winter felt like it was in full swing. Fortunately we encountered some awesome Trail Magic from two sets of Trail Angels who had generously put us up in their houses for 3 nights, fed us and shuttled us to trailheads.

On the morning of November 26th, a small group of us was savoring the last few moments of indoor heating at our Trail Angel's house. We discussed the approaching snowstorm and its potential ramifications if it were to hit us on the Trail. Ultimately, we decided winter weather was inevitable and not worth waiting on. We either needed to thicken our skin and persevere these last few hundred miles or go home. We loaded up into the van and headed to the trailhead well aware of the possibility of snow.

It was raining slightly as we got out of the van. The drizzle quickly turned into a heavy rain. By the time we reached the shelter several hours later, we were drenched to the bone. We had only hiked 11 miles. A miserable and shivering 11 miles. It was 34 degrees outside and only going to get colder as the sun set.

Five of us snuggled up in the shelter that night nervously laughing about having to put our cold wet clothes back on the next morning.

The storm hit and woke everyone up around 3 AM. Snow was blowing in hard from the open wall of the shelter. My buddy's feet had been covered. We latched down a tarp as an additional shelter wall to prevent the worst of it from mounting up inside. The tarp flapped and cracked like a whip for hours.

It was eerily quiet when we woke up. Everything was frozen, especially our wet clothes from the day before. I can remember cracking my brittle socks into a 'V' shape and spinning them like an icy dreidel on the shelter's table. A rock helped me break in my shoes and laces enough to weasel my foot inside. The nearest lodging was 17 miles away. It was going to be a long day.

I quickly realized that this was one of the most beautiful natural landscapes I had ever scene. Every leaf, branch and grass blade was covered in a thick white blanket. The woods were still and more silent than I had ever heard. I mean, *silent*. No birds chirping, no breeze, nothing... just the grey sky shape shifting overhead.

It was a winter wonderland. It was ours.

Despite the cold conditions, we all had a positive attitude and enjoyed the beauty of the hike. We hydrated by eating piles of snow on the tree branches. It almost became a competition to see who could have the best 'beard-cicle' - or longest icicles forming from their beard. We laughed, threw snowballs and trudged through the virgin snow.

The snow piled over our knees on the ridgelines forcing us to lift each leg twice as high. Trees hung low from the weight of the snow forcing us to, at times, get on all fours and crawl. We always enjoyed the pile of snow falling down our necks as we stood back up.

Every mile was exhausting. 17 miles later, we reached the small group of cabins for rent and passed out with the heater on full blast.

Springer.

As a Southbounder, I ended my thru-hike on top of Springer Mountain on the afternoon of December 17th.

That last morning was surreal. I loaded up my gear and was ready to crush the final stretch. Only 15.1 miles to Springer. The anticipation was killing me. It had been 6 months of intense hiking and over a decade since I first considered thru-hiking the Appalachian Trail.

The end was SO CLOSE.

My body had taken a serious beating - my feet in particular. I had lost half of my toenails and relied on an intricate webbing of band aids, duct tape and Vaseline to prevent anymore blisters from forming or, at least minimize the bleeding from the existing ones.

My right heel had been going in and out of severely numbing pain. My experience with stress fractures led me to believe I was very close to being in a boot brace for 8 weeks.

The 0 degree nights had been too much for my 15 degree sleeping bag. I utilized anything that had any potential insulating powers. Every piece of cloth, including my tent and tarp, were layered and acted as my nightly cocoon. Even then, some nights were too cold to sleep through. My eyes had been twitching for weeks - a textbook sign of sleep exhaustion.

The idea of taking a hot bath and then sleeping in a bed in cotton sheets was intoxicating. I frequently thought about dipping each one of my numb and swollen toes into a hot tub. I could almost feel the warm water coax each knuckle as my foot slowly became entirely submerged.

I opened up the trail log at the shelter for a quick entry before getting through this last day. There were lots of entries from fellow hiking friends either days or weeks ahead. Their comments ranged from being miserably exhausted to uncontrollably excited. All of them, however, reflected on their hike and what it had meant to them.

It became clear that the end of the Trail was the end of a whole lot more - the end of an amazing experience, the end of my new friends and comrades, the end of submerging myself in nature. This was goodbye.

I wrote my last log entry as a thru-hiker and set off on the trail. My worries faded away along with the feet pain, cold bones, hunger, exhaustion, everything.

It wasn't until I actually saw the sign on Springer that it hit me. I literally collapsed to my knees, kissed the trail marker and cried. It was one of the most emotional moments of my life.

A strong sense of accomplishment and pride along with a turmoil of sadness and confusion filled me. I was so happy to have persevered through all of the obstacles, yet so sad to be departing from my recent home.

CHAPTER 2

You Should Be Excited

Before we jump into the nitty gritty, I want you to be excited about what awaits your thru-hike.

Experience Unparalleled Acts of Kindness (giving AND receiving).
You will experience some amazing generosity with no expectations of anything in return. Strangers will offer you a ride, a place to stay, a home cooked meal, anything. You might be surprised to find yourself letting your guard down and paying it forward.

Get in Super Human Shape.
You can almost guarantee weight loss. You will turn into a lean hiking machine able to walk 'mountain marathons' day in and day out. You will probably be the best shape of your life... and lower some stress levels.

Feel Alive.
There are few things in my life that felt as real or as 'in the moment' as hiking the Appalachian Trail. Bang your chest and roar on top of mountains.

Become a Backpacking Guru.
You will sleep outside for nearly half a year. Being outside
for 6 months is probably more than most 'survival experts'
ever have. You will be an outdoor and backpacking gear
expert.

Forget What Day It Is.
Other than making sure the post office is not closed, the
days of the week will blur together. Is it Tuesday or
Saturday? I dunno, don't care and neither does anyone
else. Say goodbye to living for the weekend and the
Monday to Friday grind.

Sleep With the Sun.
No alarm clocks. Back to the good 'ole caveman days. Sun
rises, you wake up. Sun sets, you sleep. The term 'hiker
midnight' refers to how early hikers usually go to sleep.
After all, there is no electricity out there and you don't
want to drain your precious headlamp battery. You're
exhausted as well so get some rest.

Stargaze Like You've Seen In The Movies.
You'll be outside most nights. Some will be on open ridge
lines with clear views of the night sky. Goodbye big city
light pollution. Shooting stars abound.

Observe Spectacular Animals.
Wild Moose, rattlesnakes, bald eagles, porcupines, grouse,
turkeys, deer, black bears, coyotes, raccoons, peregrine
falcons, mice, salamanders, turtles, bull frogs, fruit bats,
red foxes, boars, copperheads, toads and several types of
owls to name a few.

Eat Wild Blueberries.
Yea… they're all over the place in summer. Get a taste of that organic, non-GMO, gluten-free, soy-free, whatever yumminess.

Meet Your Best Friends.
You will meet some awesome people from all over the country… and some from other countries. Everyone has different interests, backgrounds, and their own reasons for hiking. All of them have made some sort of sacrifice to pursue this journey and actually do it. Sharing an experience as unique and dramatic as the AT can build lifelong friendships and strong camaraderie.

Disconnect From Tech.
You'll never meet a group of people more excited to not have cell phone reception. For that matter, you probably won't even see many cell phones. You mean no texting and no Facebook?! Well, you can in town. Block out those interruptions while on the trail though.

Enjoy The Bare Necessities.
Live simply. Your life boils down to about 40 items on your back. Let that soak in for a minute. No wallet or car keys in your pockets. No deciding what to wear every morning. This is it. You will quickly learn how little you really need in life. Mo' money, mo' problems, right?

Go Slow.
Go everywhere at 2 miles per hour. No speeding in your car or hurrying in the morning to get to work. You are walking. Rushing means running which is not realistic. Chill out and slow down. The first thing I noticed after the AT was the pace of a car. They were so FAST. The trees

passed by like machine gun fire.

Learn the Forest.
You will become familiar with forests, plants, and trees.
Most of the US is covered in 'new growth' or secondary
forest which means it has been cut down at some point in
history. Parts of the AT go through 'old growth' forests
which have never been disturbed by logging. They feel
prehistoric. I had never stopped to pay attention to forest
types prior to the AT. The differences are dramatic.

Drink Natural Water.
Have you ever drunk from anything other than a water
bottle or the tap? You will almost always drink from a
stream or pond or river on the trail... filtered first, of
course. Cool, fresh mountain water is pretty amazing.

Embrace the Unknown.
Adventure is somewhat defined by the unknown. You
don't know what is around the next turn of the trail, who
you are going to meet, or what you might encounter.
Completely new experiences.

Feel Free.
Break your societal routine. You will wake up with no
agenda other than to put one foot in front of the other. No
meetings, no bills, no errands, just hiking. Feel free to stop
and enjoy that overlook, make a fire and stare at the stars,
sleep in - whatever you want and whenever you want.
Maybe you'll stay an extra day in town and checkout that
brewery.

Hit the Refresh Button.
You may suffer from personal issues (a lost loved one,

divorce, addiction, etc.) and seek inner peace and solitude. You may just want to take a break and assess the next chapter of your life. Either way, the Appalachian Trail is a great time to take a step outside your regular life and reflect.

Forget About Politics.
You won't watch any of your favorite sports teams play or follow the most recent political turmoil. New music and TV shows may come and go completely unnoticed. The most interesting thing is realizing how little you care.

See Scenery That'll Make You Cry.
Sunrises, sunsets, mountain tops, overlooks and meadows. Some of these views will be permanently etched into your memory and may be some of the most beautiful landscapes you'll ever see.

Experience Overwhelming Pride.
6 months and over 2,000 miles is a huge accomplishment... mentally and physically. You will feel like a boss when you finish and excited to take on new challenges in life.

CHAPTER 3

Preparation

Are You *Really* Up For It?

Alright, alright. I get it Chris. You like the AT. But, I'm not sure *I* will like the AT.

Fair enough. You may not. Plenty of people don't and that is totally cool. Let's talk about some things to consider.

Thru-hiking is a 6 month commitment. 6 months of anything demands a certain level of planning. 6 months of an entirely new way of life can be overwhelming.

Beautiful images of mountains and wildlife from the Appalachian Trail can be enough for you to say, "That looks fun, I am going to hike it!" In general, there seems to be a big disconnect between the romanticized Appalachian Trail experience and the reality of the hike. The difficulty of the hike is a rude awakening for most.

The statistics change every year. However, it is estimated that less than 25% of hikers who start out actually finish their hike. That number alone should be enough for you to consider how difficult the AT is and to take this planning process seriously.

The AT does not care how tired you are or how bad the weather is. You still tie your shoes and hike.

Ever seen the movie, *Goodfellas*? There is a scene where the gangster, Henry Hill, describes their gang's policy on collecting outstanding payments from clients.

"Business bad? F#$! you, pay me.
Oh, you had a fire? F#$! you, pay me.
Place got hit by lightning, huh? F#$! you, pay me!"

While not as life-threatening, the AT can be as equally demanding.

"Snowing outside? F#$! you, hike.
Ankle swelled up like an orange? F#$! you, hike.
Thirsty and the stream is dry? F#$! you, hike!"

There are seemingly countless formidable reasons that have the potential to force you off trail before completion.

The most common possibilities:
- Stress Related Injury: fractures, swelling, blisters, aches, etc.
- Accidental Injury: slips, falls, sprains, gashes, tears, etc.
- Sickness: Lyme disease (ticks), Giardia (unfiltered water), Norovirus (stomach bug), etc.
- Misery: too cold, too hot, too tired, too hungry, too wet, too uncomfortable.

- Boredom: burned out from hiking all day every day.
- No Money: poor financial planning.
- Causeless: Why in the hell am I doing this?
- Family: emergency or homesick.

Other than a family emergency, I feel like all of these can be avoided by preparing adequately. Ask yourself *"Is this something I really want to do?"*

If so, then the goal of this is to help you prepare for your thru-hike and hopefully put some nerves at ease. We can break this preparation phase down into three categories: mental, physical, and financial.

Optimism and Mental Framework.

A strong mental framework is the single most important factor to ensure you have a successful thru-hike. You consistently hear about how hard an AT thru-hike is. No doubt. It is hard. Hiking up mountains all day is freaking tough.

It Will Suck (at times).
I was miserable several times on my thru-hike. I experienced some of the most extreme sensations of my life on the Trail. The hungriest I have ever been, the coldest I have ever been, the most physically exhausted I have ever been, the most bored I have ever been, etc.

The monotony of hiking everyday certainly affected my happiness as well. Seeing trees and more trees day in and day out took a toll. Not every day was full of dramatic landscapes and beautiful wildlife. In fact, most were not. While I did meet some amazing characters and develop great friendships, there were plenty of days where I just wanted my own space. I could also fill up a whole chapter on every little ankle twist, slippery fall, bleeding blister and itchy bug bite. To put it bluntly, the Trail can really suck sometimes.

You must have a strong mental framework to combat the potential struggles. I have a few suggestions...

Find Your Motivation.
'Why am I out here? This is not as beautiful as the photos nor as fun as my buddy had said.'

I listed some stuff to motivate you to consider the hike earlier. Here is an outline of some general reasons why people decide to take the plunge:
- Freedom.
- Adventure.
- Friends.
- Health.
- Challenge.
- Nature.
- Escape.
- Simple Living.

Understanding why you are hiking is HUGE. Having a clear 'mission' can be a great combatant on less-than-joyful days. I suggest you write down a list of several concrete reasons why you want to hike the AT.

Find Your "Why Nots".
Assess the opportunity cost. In other words, what are you

going to miss out on over the next 6 months?

You are definitely going to have to make some sacrifices. You are essentially saying goodbye to everything you know. You will be, for the most part, disconnected from the real world. If anything new and noteworthy happens, you probably won't know until you reach town several days later.

There may be some important family events you will have to decline. Maybe a good friend's wedding or the birth of a nephew.

When I was about 12 years old, my father gave me a quote from Theodore Roosevelt printed on a piece of construction paper. It was a section from the "Man in the Arena" speech.

It is not the critic who counts... The credit belongs to the man who is actually in the arena, whose face is marred by dust and sweat and blood; who strives valiantly; who errs, who comes short again and again, because there is no effort without error and shortcoming; but who does actually strive to do the deeds; who knows great enthusiasms, the great devotions; who spends himself in a worthy cause; who at the best knows in the end the triumph of high achievement, and who at the worst, if he fails, at least fails while daring greatly, so that his place shall never be with those cold and timid souls who neither know victory nor defeat.

For me, *not hiking* the AT was the biggest sacrifice. I could live my comfortable life listing countless reasons why it was not the right time to hike. There are always going to be reasons not to do anything. What if I took that leap though? I could plan and save for months and then fail. I'd be such a joke. Well… so what? As Teddy Roosevelt triumphantly says, at least I would 'strive to do the deeds' and not join 'those cold and timid souls who neither know victory nor defeat'.

To some degree, I just had to commit and then take the necessary steps. Family events could wait 6 months. Committing to this hike was important to me despite what I might miss out on. Interestingly enough, I started to realize how little I cared about anything in the real world. I became impartial to politics and pop culture almost entirely. It was liberating.

Think Long Term.
Ever written a book, raised kids, started a business, studied for a big exam, or trained for a race? I bet all of those can suck at times. But, I'd bet the reward is worth the strife. Anything worth achieving is tough. The AT is no different.

This experience will go down as one of your most proud moments, experiences, and achievements. Think about how you will feel when you finish and for years to come.

What if the hike was not 'strife' though and you could enjoy the process of attempting the achievement?

Whoa ho ho. That'd be a win win, right?

Find Your Daily Enjoyments and Gratitude's.
Don't make the Trail harder than it is. Don't fight it; embrace it. Any challenge is probably a good test and going to make you stronger after conquering it.

This is about staying positive. At the end of the day, my hiking partners and I would often list out what we called 'Rose, Bud, Thorn'. Rose; what we were thankful for that day. Bud; what we were looking forward to. Thorn; what sucked or could have been better or what we would like to improve.

You can be thankful for that sweet candy bar after dinner or maybe the sunshine on your face after so many rainy days or maybe that incident that gave you a good deep belly laugh. You can look forward to a hot shower in the next trail town or maybe reading your book tomorrow night. You can wish your feet had been less sore or maybe you would like to have seen the black bear that everyone else saw.

Not only was this a great social exercise to communicate how everyone was doing, but it was an opportunity to reflect on the day. As time went on, I found myself counting what I was thankful for throughout the day. Everything could be viewed in a positive light. The sopping wet rain can help rinse the dirt off your face. The wet firewood can help sharpen your fire-starting skills. The scorching hot day can help dry out your wet socks.

Everyone I hiked with felt pretty comfortable and confident in their hike and never seemed to get into a miserable hiking grind. It was much more about enjoying the experience than bitching about pains and inconveniences. I honestly never reached a point where I thought "okay, this is just too terrible… not sure I can keep going."

Quitting Time.
If you are miserable for an extended period of time, then get out of there! Months of misery will not be fun nor make you feel proud after completion.

If you do reach a quitting point, I ask for you to consider two things:

- Am I just having a bad day? You may just be exhausted and need to take a zero day.
- Will I regret leaving? Maybe you just need to change up a few things (new hiking group, etc) and can press on.

I feel like most people who quit do so very early on. In other words, if you make it a couple hundred miles, the likelihood that you will make it to 2,000 is much higher.

Getting in Shape.

Super Human Machine.
You will be hiking a lot. Let's actually break down how much. I'm going to round up to an even 2,200 miles for the length of the Trail. Depending on your pace and terrain, you will hike roughly 2 miles an hour. Therefore, you will hike an estimated 1,100 hours total on your thru-hike.

Let's say you want to finish within 22 weeks (5 and a half months). That means you will hike an average of 50 hours per week. You will be in motion, actually hiking, over 8 hours a day for 6 days a week. I hate to even mention the word 'job' in a time of unemployed freedom. But, you are about to take on hiking as a full-time position.

Continuing with this 22 week time frame... you will average 100 miles per week. Here is what your typical week will look like:

Day 1: 20 miles
Day 2: 17 miles
Day 3: 13 miles
Day 4: 20 miles
Day 5: 17 miles
Day 6: 13 miles
Day 7: Rest

Sure, these are obviously rough estimates. However, you need to understand just how much physical stress you are putting on your body every day for an extended period of time.

Understandably, physical conditioning is one of the most common questions asked when preparing for a thru-hike. My answer, *how on earth can you train for hiking 8 hours a day for 6 months other than just doing it?*

There is nothing inherently 'hard' about hiking. I hiked a section with 'El Flaco'. He was on his 3rd AT thru-hike and was frequently asked "Wow, how do you do it?" He always shrugged it off, "I put one foot in front of the other."

I knew plenty of people that started off in less-than-Spartan-like shape. The general consensus is that most people condition as they go. That being said, I do have a few thoughts and concerns about starting the Trail Homer-Simpson-style.

Listen to Your Body.
Please start off slow and listen to your body. Maybe do 5 miles a day for the first couple of days. If you are not sore, then pick it up. If you are, then slow down and be patient as your body adjusts to the new physical demands. It generally takes several weeks, if not months, to be conditioned to hike 15 miles per day.

The worst mistake you can make is start off too hard (just like I did on Day 1) and get an injury that sends you home only a few weeks into your hike. All the logistical planning, time and money spent on gear, and anticipation for an epic hike could be wasted because you got antsy. This is not a race to the finish line so don't stress if you have a slow start. There is a saying on the Trail "last one to finish, wins".

If you are concerned about starting out like Jabba the Hut, let's lay out a very basic suggested physical condition. As a general rule of thumb, I like to ask people if they can jog a mile. 'Jog' is an ambiguous and subjective term that can range from an 8 to 20 minute mile. However, you probably already know right now if you can jog a mile. It is faster than a walk and not quite a full on run. If you cannot comfortably jog a mile, then I would suggest setting that as a prerequisite goal before setting out on your thru-hike.

It'll Hurt.
Beyond the sheer physical exertion of a thru-hike, your body will take on new levels of stress. Your body is not used to carrying a heavy pack up and down steep mountains every day. In particular, your knees, feet, ankles, shoulders, and back are subject to big aches and pains.

Make sure your gear fits well and feels good ahead of time. Otherwise, there is not much you can do to prepare for those stresses.

By the end of the Trail, I was wearing a knee brace and two ankle braces. I was actually starting to have tendinitis in my elbows for putting too much weight on my trekking poles. My Iliotibial Band (ligament that runs down your leg on the outside of your knee) was sore off and on as well forcing me to do 'log rolls' to stretch it out many mornings. I also bought some compression socks to help with shin splints.

Some people are totally fine without any braces. Trying to anticipate your muscle pains is very difficult. Unless you know you have a weak spot, I suggest picking up a brace in trail towns on an as needed basis.

You're Not Too (insert excuse).
I hiked with a 70 year old man with Parkinson's Disease who shook so much he could barely hold on to his trekking poles, a 5 year old, and a bionic man with metal appendages. If you are concerned about health issues, check in with the doctor before heading out.

Prepping the Homefront.

Going All In?
I quit my job and sold most of my possessions before my thru-hike. This took several months, if not a year, of planning and saving. That being said, I was on the extreme end of the spectrum. You don't have to go 'all in', quit your job and sell your house in a blaze of glory. Let's break it down.

Take Care of Your Job.
Packing up and hitting the trail for 6 months is probably
not going to please your boss which is why you will find
most hikers in a transitional phase in life - either right out
of college, in between jobs or recently retired. Some decide
to quit their jobs entirely. Some have worked out a leave of
absence with their employer or a sabbatical. The vast
majority are unemployed though (or shall we say
'funemployed'?).

Is quitting your job really that scary?
Or do you think you won't be able to find another one?

For me, hiking actually created more career opportunities
than it destroyed. I started a backpacking food business
after the Trail and continue to travel the world full time.

Take Care of Your Possessions.
- House/ Apartment. You have a lot of options. Sell
  it (and your mortgage!). Lease it. Sublease it. Have
  a friend or family member take care of it for free
  or for a discount. Planning ahead can also help
  you phase out your lease.
- Car. Same thing. You can sell it or rent it or have a
  friend turn it on every month to make sure the
  battery still works.
- Personal Items. Furniture, television, appliances,
  etc. You can sell them at a garage sale or on
  Craigslist, give them away, or put them into
  storage. Store it in a friend's basement or attic or
  rent a storage unit. You might enjoy a big purge
  though!

Eliminate Services and Automate Payments.
There are a lot of other financial factors to consider. Debt, phone bills, health care, etc. You may need a family member or friend to handle some of these payments. I suggest canceling as many services and subscriptions as possible. For anything remaining, set up automated online payments. You want to be free from financial worries. I phased out my phone contract and made sure not to sign up for credit cards. The post office can hold your mail.

Managing the Kids.
Thru-hiking with kids is probably the toughest thing to manage and just might not work. It is illegal to sell your offspring and, in addition to the moral dilemma, probably not a good idea. However, I hiked with several individual parents with kids back at home or actually with them on the Trail. Some ideas:

- Spend 1 week at home every month. This would be logistically taxing. But, could be a great option to check back in with the family every 3 weeks. Might be nice to rest as well.
- Are you able to leave your other half with the kids? Some people hire nannies or bring in the grandparents to support the home front.
- Section Hike. Take a few weeks or months every summer to hike a large piece of the AT.
- Bring the kids along. You can do it in summer when they are out of school. Some families also had homeschooling arrangements setup.
- Wait until they turn 18 and are out of the house. The problem here, of course, is this could be in many, many years.

Keep Costs in Perspective.
People often surprisingly ask "How can you afford to hike for that long?!" Thru-hiking is actually relatively inexpensive compared to what you would spend in 6 months in the real world. Depending on what part of the country you live in, a thru-hike probably costs the equivalent to only a few months' rent. In my adult life, I spent the least amount of money per month while hiking the AT. No rent, no electricity, no gas.

Budgeting.

Too many people get off trail and quit because they run out of funds. This should not happen to you. A little planning and basic budgeting, and you'll be fine.

Here we go again with some numbers. The four main expenses are as follows and in this order: Food, gear, lodging, and logistics. Here is an estimate on my expenses.

Food.
Trail: $10/ day X 150 days = $1,500
Town: $25/ day X 30 days = $600

I ate very well in town and recommend you do the same. You will need the nutrition and enjoy feasting on non-trail food. As far as drinking, I had an occasional beer. But, I was not a heavy drinker. You should probably budget more here if you are a partier.

Gear.
Tent/ Shelter = $250
Sleeping Bag = $150

Backpack = $150
Mid-layer Jacket = $100
Shell Jacket = $100
Sleeping Pad = $100
Shoes = $100
Stove/ Kitchen = $60
Bag Liner = $50
Water Filter = $40
Headlamp = $40
Trekking Poles = $35
Stuff Sacks = $30
Water Containers = $20
Other = $150
Total = $1,375

Early planning allowed me to prey on off season gear and really shop around for the best deals.

Accommodation.
Hostel: $15/ night X 30 nights = $450
You can split a hotel room with people in trail towns. I knew many hikers that would camp right outside of town to save money as well. Personally, I really appreciated cotton sheets and a hot shower when I could get them.

Logistics.
Airfare/ shuttles = $300

A flight to Atlanta, GA (or Bangor, ME) and probably a bus or shuttle from there to the trail head. Don't forget a return flight as well. Hitchhiking (and hiking!) will take care of the rest of your transportation.

Total Cost of My Thru-Hike: $4,225

This budget can vary A LOT depending on what gear you already have, eating and drinking habits, lodging needs, etc. The real budget-minded hikers might be able to squeeze by with $3,000, while the more luxurious hikers may spend up to $7,000.

If you had to pin me down to one number for the cost of a thru-hike, I would advise you to set aside $5,000. This will provide a comfortable hike - quality gear, decent lodging, adequate food, and a small cushion to fall back on.

Cash Cushion.
I'll admit it was stressful not knowing what kind of job I would come back to. Adding an extra cash cushion to my budget helped me gain some peace of mind though. Worst case, I knew I could live off of that cushion (or with my parents... which I did) while looking for a job and waiting for a stable income again. If you are really going to be counting pennies, I recommend having a similar cash cushion or outline a realistic path back to employment.

How to Request a Sponsorship.

Reach out to your favorite gear brands before leaving for some potential gear on the house. It never hurts to ask.

Disclaimer. You must use this for GOOD, not exploitation.

Unless you are breaking records or have a huge online following, it will be hard to get any cash from a company for your journey. It is, however, very realistic to get some free gear from an outdoor brand.

Before my thru-hike, I spent an afternoon reaching out to nearly 50 gear companies and received some really great gear from several of them.

To pitch an outdoor brand, you need to think about what is in it for *them*... and be willing to follow through with the offer. My company (Greenbelly Meals) gets a ton of donation and sponsorship requests. I'd love to help everyone out, but we would go out of business if we said yes to them all. I'm sure other outdoor brands are no different and must prioritize giving away free product. Many companies don't provide free gear at all or have a lengthy sponsorship application process that takes months to get reviewed and approved.

Your pitch should be...

1. Short. Whoever is reading this is busy and gets pitched a lot.
2. Personalized. Do not copy and paste the exact same template for each brand. It will be obvious and probably get trashed. Be yourself, appreciative and not overly spammy.
3. Have a Great Offer. Shipping free gear costs money and they want to know why you are worth it.
4. Have a Clear Offer. Make it easy for them to know exactly what you are looking for.

Here is an example of a pitch I would send...

Hey (company name),

I thought you might be interested in getting involved with my upcoming 6 month hike of the Appalachian Trail. Things I can offer you:

- *Video review and mentions on my YouTube channel which I will be updating every week.*
- *A product review on my blog like this (link example) which gets XXXX monthly visits.*
- *No less than 10 product shots from the AT. See a few attached examples of my portfolio.*
- *Test any potential new products and provide detailed feedback.*

I leave on March 15th and would love a (product name). Shipping address is below. Happy with anything you can spare though :)

Either way, thanks for the consideration! Cheers,

Chris Cage (555-123-4567)
Main Street 123
Awesomeville, USA 12345

CHAPTER 4

Logistics

Direction.

Before deciding when to go, decide the direction you want
to go. Hiking in winter is brutal. Therefore, you want to
hit the warmest 5-6 month window of the year.

Your options:

NOBO.
Northbound = Georgia to Maine. Roughly 90% of all thru-
hikers go north. NOBOs start at Springer Mountain, GA in
early spring and end at Mt. Katahdin in late summer. They
hike with the blossoming spring flowers. The first day of
spring is a popular day to start. I'd recommend starting
anywhere between March 1 - 30 though.

Pros
- Large social groups. 50 thru-hikers might be
within a day of you. You will get to know a lot
people and possibly have more options to find
who you enjoy hiking with.

- Start off easy. GA is a great primer.
- More infrastructure. Everything revolves around the NOBO season. Hostels, outfitters, shuttles, etc. We (SOBOs) heard stories of elaborate trail magic cookouts setup at road crossings for NOBOs.
- Epic finish. Mt. Katahdin is an iconic summit.

Cons

- Crowded shelters and overbooked hostels.
- Less solitude in nature.
- Potentially snowy start in early March.
- Mt. Katahdin closes down on October 15th for weather concerns. This may put you in a time crunch if you start in late April.

SOBO.

Southbound = Maine to Georgia. About 10% go south. SOBOs start at Mt. Katahdin, ME in early summer and end at Springer Mountain, GA in late fall. They hike with the bright fall foliage. I recommend starting at the northern terminus anytime from June 1 - 30.

I started June 13th and wish I would have started more like June 1. I found winter especially harsh. An extra couple weeks would have been a nice cushion to prevent from hitting that intense snowy weather down South.

Pros

- Intimate social groups. Hike with maybe a handful of thru-hikers at a time. As a SOBO, I am biased. But, I suspect I would not have enjoyed the large NOBO group environment.
- More solitude in nature.
- Epic start. Mt. Katahdin on Day 1. I also thought

Maine and New Hampshire were some of the most beautiful sections.
- No deadline. There is no one preventing you from finishing at Springer in the dead of winter. The cold weather should be enough of a deadline for you though.

Cons

- Lack of infrastructure. Not too common. But, there were several parks and hostels that were closed for the season as I hiked later into fall and early winter.
- The 100 Mile Wilderness is immediately after Mt. Katahdin. While extremely flat (and gorgeous), it can be a rude awakening for rationing food and supplies properly. Other than a few logging roads, once you start the Wilderness, you must finish it.
- Hard start. ME and NH are beautiful. But they have the toughest terrain and most drastic elevation changes on the entire AT.
- Black flies. NOBOs certainly encounter their fair share of bugs. But, the black flies in Maine in June are hellacious.

Flip Flop.
Hike north or south to the halfway point (typically Harpers Ferry, WV). Then get transportation to the other end of the Trail and hike the second half. You can hike with the best of the seasons by doing this and avoid cold weather almost entirely. However, extra transportation will be more expensive and you will not find many flip-flopper's to share your journey with.

Section Hike.
Common for people unable to commit several continuous months of their life to a thru-hike. You hike small sections at a time over many years. I hiked with several section hikers who viewed each new section as their vacation and the AT as their annual pilgrimage.

Getting to the Trail Head.

Springer Mountain, GA.
There is no parking lot on top of Springer. Therefore, you need to get dropped off at a nearby road or parking lot in order to reach the official starting summit point (for NOBOs). Most hikers actually begin their hike 8.8 miles farther south at Amicalola Falls. This stretch in between Amicalola Falls and Springer Mountain is also known as the "Approach Trail".

Fly into Atlanta, GA. From there, you need to get to Amicalola State Park or a nearby city like Gainesville, GA. There are a lot of public transportation options (buses, Amtrak, MARTA). Hiker Hostel offers shuttle pickups from either Gainesville, GA or the North Springs MARTA Station. They have a package that includes a bunk and a shuttle to the trailhead the next morning as well.

Mt. Katahdin, ME.
Similar to Springer, there is no parking lot on top of Mt. Katahdin. You will need to get dropped off at Baxter State Park and hike 5 miles north to the starting summit point (for SOBOs) and backtrack that same 5 miles to the parking lot to continue southbound.

Fly into Bangor, ME. From there, you need to get to Baxter State Park or a nearby city like Millinocket, ME. I took an hour long bus ride from Bangor to Medway and then had a half hour shuttle to the hostel in Millinocket (The Appalachian Trail Lodge). The hostel picked me up at the bus stop in Medway, provided a bunk and then a shuttle to trailhead the next morning.

Navigating the Trail.

Map and Compass.
Simply put - you don't need 'em. 99% of the Trail is pretty obvious and marked by "blaze's" every 50-100 yards. AT blazes are 2x6 inch white stripes of paint located near eye-level, typically on a tree. To mark the trail in treeless areas (balds, rocky tops, pastures, etc.), there may be manmade posts with the white blaze or a pile of rocks, known as cairns.

Guide Books.
Simply put - you need one. There are two main options that are often scrutinized and compared down to the finest detail. Big picture, they both provide adequate info so don't over analyze this decision.

The A.T. Guide by David Miller is what I went with. It provides a horizontal profile of the entire Trail. Having detailed trail gradient info and elevation measurements is SUPER HELPFUL. Not only does it inform you how difficult or easy the upcoming miles are, but about upcoming water sources and shelters. Complete with hostel, shuttle, town info and a bunch of other good stuff.

<u>Appalachian Trail Thru-Hiker's Companion</u> from The Appalachian Trail Conservancy provides the same useful elevation profile and landmarks. The landmarks are on separate pages though which, for some hikers, is more organized. Personally, I would not like flipping back and forth to reference. This guide also provides a bit more info and history about the landmarks, which is something I would have really enjoyed.

Phone Apps.
These could take over the printed guide books mentioned above in future years. Apps like Guthooks provide similar elevation profiles and trail points of interest as the printed guides. They can also operate in airplane mode (aka - you can download the maps and operate offline without any mobile or internet connection). The commenting feature allows hikers to update certain points of interests as well - dry water sources, overbooked hostels, etc.

The big problem for me is the whole *phone* aspect. I don't want to fiddle with my phone all day long and worry about the battery life. However, if you are already carrying a phone and can ration the battery life, these are great.

GPS, PLBs and Satellite.
Meh. May add a lot of weight. The AT is not remote enough either to require an emergency beacon. There are several satellite options out there that pinpoint your location or can be used to send short messages in areas without phone reception (see Spot or DeLorme products). This can be particularly useful for blogging or allowing family and friends to track your progress. My mom insisted I carry a personal locater beacon (PLB) in case I

needed to send out a distress signal. Thankfully, I convinced her it was unnecessary after my first leg. Thanks Mama.

Getting to Town.

Hike.
The Trail goes directly through a few small towns. Yea, as in you will see a white blaze on the sidewalk. Other times, it might be a 20 minute walk down the road. Most often though, the town is several miles away and you need a ride from a shuttle or hitchhike.

Hostel Shuttles.
Sometimes available if you are staying at the hostel. These require planning ahead of time though and are not a reliable option.

Hitchhike.
The most common option. When I tell people that I hitchhiked on the AT, they act like I am telling them that I shower with my parents. Hitchhiking is just absurd to most Americans. They think of kidnappings and horrific rape and murder tales. Prior to the AT, I had been exposed to hitchhiking in New Zealand where it is still common and viewed as an economical and environmentally friendly means of transportation. The AT is no different.

Hitchhiking is the most common method to get to town. If hitchhiking is absurd to you - just hold on a sec. I am not peer pressuring you into thinking all the cool kids are doing it nor that it is 100% safe. You are, of course, taking a risk when hopping into a car with a stranger. However, almost all thru-hikers hitchhike. The citizens near the Trail are used to driving by trail crossings and seeing hikers waiting. Your driver has probably picked up many hikers for many years.

I met some amazing people hitchhiking and experienced some humbling random acts of kindness. Several times I was dripping wet in the cold rain and someone graciously picked me. The driver might have an old car rusted to the bone or a new luxurious wagon with sleek leather interior. People didn't seem to care how dirty I was. They were just happy to help someone and enjoyed being a part of the AT community.

If you are terrified about hitchhiking, here are a few safety tips and considerations:

- Don't do it alone. Hitchhike with a buddy or a few people. This will give you a physical sense of safety and also deter anyone who *might* have bad intentions.
- Prescreen your driver before getting in the car. I hate to use the word 'judge'. But, if the driver seems like a drunken lunatic, have a backup excuse plan. Tell him or her you just got to the trailhead and are still waiting for a few friends to catch up. Another idea, you are waiting for a shuttle or a friend to come pick you up soon.
- You can always carry a small thing of mace or pepper spray.
- Hitchhike in daylight.

Some other, non-safety related, hitchhiking tips.

- You will smell horrible and your driver may immediately regret picking you up. Be considerate and offer to keep the windows down and put your pack in the trunk. For this reason, truck beds are always my favorite way to hitch.

- Change into your camp clothes at the trail crossing. You will look more presentable and less likely to bring grime into the driver's car.
- If possible, hitchhike with a girl. I felt like a female helped soften the group's image and appear less threatening to the driver.
- Make it easy for the driver to stop. Be on the correct side of the road with enough distance for them to see you in advance and think about whether or not they want to stop.
- You can carry a sign. A permanent marker and a pizza box worked well.

Resupplying.

You will resupply your food about every 3 to 7 days. Some sections, like Maine, are very remote and can have limited resupply options. Other sections, like Massachusetts, are relatively urban and have frequent trail crossings and easy access to towns.

Gas Stations.

At trail crossings, there is often a gas station or restaurant or mini mart to grab some snacks, a hot meal or just a cold drink. You might need to hike a few hundred yards down the road to reach it. In some towns, a gas station may be your only resupply option (hello Beef Jerky!). To get a proper resupply though, you will need to access a reasonable sized grocery store which are usually several miles from the trail crossing.

Stores and Outfitters.

Most towns will have a grocery store to stock up your food for the next leg of your hike... until the next town with another resupply. There are several outfitters scattered along the Trail as well to replace any worn or broken gear.

Mail Drops.

Not as common, but you can pre plan all of your food and strategically ship it to Post Offices in trail towns. They will hold it for free until you pick it up. Many hostels offer this service as well, often for a fee though. This allows you to budget, ration quantities and order a large variety of food. An example Post Office mailing label:

Chris Cage (or "Smooth")
PLEASE HOLD FOR A.T. HIKER
General Delivery
City, State Zip Code

Mail drops can be tricky and extremely inflexible. Your dietary needs and taste buds will probably be different than you planned for prior to departing. Also, mail drops force you to stop at each of those specific towns and arrive when the post office is open. I remember shipping new hiking shoes to a post office and arriving late Saturday afternoon. I had to wait in town until they opened up again on Monday morning.

Bounce Boxes.

I found these to be a good mail drop compromise. Instead of trying to plan my entire resupply months in advance, bounce boxes let you ship supplies up a week or two on an as needed basis. Within a week or two window, you have a MUCH better idea of where you will be and when.

Put the supplies you need (but don't necessarily need ON the Trail) into a box and ship it forward to the next town. Repeat as needed. This was particularly helpful if I bought a 10 pack of granola bars and only needed 6 for the upcoming section or if I bought a 4 pack of batteries and only needed 2. At times, I also bounced the 'sometimes needed' items ahead like extra socks, my journal, seasonal medicine or my ankle brace.

Hiker Boxes.
A box of freebies. Generally leftover food or gear from previous hikers often located in hostels or shelters. Not reliable enough to count on as a resupply. But, you can be sure to find (and leave behind) useful items. A packet of noodles, spare batteries, etc.

Permits and Regulations.

You do not need a permit to hike the AT. There are, however, two sections through national parks that require a permit to camp: Great Smoky Mountain National Park and Shenandoah National Park. You can get your permits in the trail towns nearby or online before entering the Parks.

I recommend registering your thru-hike online with the Appalachian Trail Conservancy. It is not required, but helps track hiker data and only takes a few minutes. They will probably send you a few free items as well.

The weather conditions in the White Mountains (section in

New Hampshire) can be dangerous and, as a safety precaution, the Appalachian Mountain Club (AMC) requires you to stay in their huts. You will more than likely be able to do a work-for-stay at them. We typically helped washed dishes for a couple hours and were allowed to sleep on the floor of the huts free-of-charge. Note these huts book up for months in advance and can be very expensive for non-thru-hikers.

CHAPTER 5

Social Hour

Demographics.

There is not really a 'typical' thru-hiker. I hiked with a wide range of people from a 5 year old on up to a 70 year old. It is about 70% male and 30% female. Everyone is out there for their own reason. I'm sure we could research some statistics on race, religion, sexual orientation. But, who really cares? The AT is a diverse bunch full of characters from all over. Discrimination is certainly not part of the AT culture and, rather on the contrary, I think hikers even pride themselves on being a very accepting and non-judging community.

Socializing.

How many people are you hiking with?
Short answer, it depends. As a SOBO, my hiking groups were generally around 2-8 people. There might be a handful more a few days ahead and a handful more a few days behind... and several handfuls in front and behind those as well. But, for the most part, there were only a few

of us at the shelters every night. NOBO groups and bubbles are several times that size. Sometimes up to 30 people groups.

How do you get rid of people you don't like?
Since there are countless factors that will affect your pace, you will probably float in and out of several hiking groups. This makes it extremely easy and flexible to meet new people and find some favorable hikers. If you are not digging that dude latching onto you, no worries. Maybe take an extra zero day in town and let that person hike on. Worst case, have a nice conversation with them and explain you want to meet some new people.

How do you communicate with fellow hikers?
Let's say you leave the shelter in the morning with another hiker. He has a slightly faster pace than you and slowly fades off up ahead. Several hours later, you still have not seen him and you are ready to stop for lunch. As you stop to take a break, you realize you and your buddy never agreed on where to meet that night. The next shelter is 5 more miles though so you assume he is there. You eat lunch and press on 5 more miles to the shelter. He is not there and the sun is setting. So... what do you do?

This kind of thing happens all of the time. Without cell phones, it can be difficult to communicate. There are a few ways to avoid this situation:

1) Plan ahead face to face. If you hike at different paces, discuss where you both want to meet at the end of the day. This will take the stress out of planning where to meet every few hours.

2) Communicate in the logbook. Logbooks (or registers) are like the Trail's cell phone. Every shelter has one. Let people know where you are going, where you have been and when. Beyond socializing, this is also a safety precaution. If you want to meet someone behind you, let them know where to meet. There could be old friends that you thought were way behind, but are actually only a few miles back. Letting hikers know where you are heading can help bottleneck all the small pockets of hikers into a specific meeting point. Example entry:

June 17, 2017 - Saw a beautiful rattlesnake this morning just before summiting Mt. Freaking Awesome. Pushed a total of 17 miles today. Legs feel like jello. Going to stay at The Doyle in Duncannon on the 20th. Cold beer, air conditioning and the most amazing time of your life awaits. Hope to see y'all there!

Smooth

Is everyone on the AT thru-hiking?
An estimated 3 million people set foot on the AT every year. However, the vast majority of these are day hikers and concentrated to a few touristy sections. Only 1,000 to 2,000 of these are thru-hikers. Thru-hikers will be who you spend the most time with. Some sections have their fair share of townies out for a weekend trip. Maybe a Boy Scout troop, etc.

Beyond that, there are section hikers who may be out there for a few days or up to several months. You also never know when someone may quit. When I reached my first Trail town in Monson, ME, I was amazed by how many people had dropped out… some I never even got to say goodbye to.

"Hike Your Own Hike".
You will hear this phrase a lot. To me, it means, this is your time and enjoy it how you wish. Don't feel pressured to put in big mile days because someone else wants to or take a side trip that you don't want to do. You planned this adventure and should experience it on your own terms.

Solo vs Group.

Hiking Solo.
- You are not 'alone'. About 90% of thru-hikers go solo. This makes it extremely easy to meet other hikers. Everyone is experiencing something new which makes the camaraderie that much more potent. Also, because everyone is alone, everyone is eager to strike up a conversation and make a friend.
- You will probably make deeper connections with new people if you go solo. You cannot rely on the crutch of an old friend for a conversation. Many hikers report 'breaking out of their shell' on their thru-hike. Not hiking with a friend could be a great social leap.
- Do what you want when you want. If you are tired, take a zero day. If you want to take a side trip, nothing is stopping you.
- Get to know yourself. You are going to spend a lot of time with YOU. I learned a lot about myself while thru-hiking. There is a unique feeling of self-reliance and 'going out on your own'.

Hiking with a Group.
- Sense of safety. The AT is super safe. Many hikers, women in particular, do not feel safe setting off into the woods alone though. Understandable. Safety, at least a stronger sense of safety, is a big reason to hike with someone.
- Consolidate your gear. Divide up your tent, stove, etc. and save a lot of space and weight.
- Mental support. Having an old friend or family member by your side can help with the daily struggles and long-term hurdles of your thru-hike.
- Share accommodation. You can always have someone to split the hotel room costs with. If you spend 20-30 nights in some sort of hotel, this savings could add up.

What to Do on the AT.

While Hiking.
- Talk. You will get to know some people very well. I mean, you may hike with someone 8 hours a day... everyday... for months. Have you spent that much time with even your closest friends?
- Listen. The woods are full of noises. Winds whistling, trees creaking, birds chirping, animals scurrying.
- Think. I often woke up with things or themes to think about for the day. What I wanted in life, what were the things that made me happy, who were some people I wanted to be sure to keep in touch with in life, what things did I want to accomplish or prioritize before I die, etc.
- Meditate. Get in the moment. Soak in your

surroundings and let your mind at ease. There are a variety of active meditation methods that you can look into.

- Audiobook. I loaded up my iPod (when those were a thing) with several audiobooks. They really helped break up the monotony of long days. Check out your local library to see if they have some free ones to download.
- Music. Again, I loaded up my iPod with a ton of music. At times, it was very helpful to boost the mood or get into a good hiking rhythm. I explored a lot of unfamiliar genres.

At Night.
- Set Camp. It takes time to unpack your sleeping pad, sleeping bag, change clothes, etc.
- Eat. Typically, dinner is the biggest meal of the day on the Trail. It is also usually the only hot meal of the day. Cooking in the morning and afternoon just takes too much time.
- Get Water. There is often a water source at the shelter. You will probably have a short walk to get there though… and then spend some more time filtering it all.
- Fire. Most hikers start off making fires every night and slowly stop after a few weeks. It just takes too much effort. In the winter though, you bet. Every night.
- Read. Most hikers are too tired to read at night. Sure, plenty of nights I was too tired as well. However, I frequently arrived to the shelter early and would read for an hour or I might just squeeze in a few minutes just before bed. I loved having an ebook to take my mind off the Trail. It

ended up being a great opportunity to read books that I otherwise would not have.

- Journal. Please, please keep a journal. You don't have to write an essay every night. Just even a few quick bullet points on your thoughts or what you saw that day. You can reflect on it for years to come. If my house were burning down and I could run in and snag only one item, it would be my journals without a doubt.
- Trail Log. Communicate with people behind you or read what those before you have written. There is always some interesting stuff in the Trail Log. Poems, stories, jokes, you name it.
- Cards. I did not carry a deck of cards because they were extra weight. Some did carry cards though and they can be a nice luxury if you arrive at a shelter early or on rainy days.
- Sleep. Let those feet air out and be sure to get some rest. Tomorrow is another big day.

In Town.

- Eat… excuse me FEAST. You don't have to worry about how heavy town food is. You also don't have to watch your waistline so eat up! You are burning more calories than you probably have in your entire life and will be barbarically hungry. Ahh, the possibilities! I always made sure to load up on fruits and veggies in town because they were significantly lacking in my apocalyptic trail diet.
- Put on Cotton. I didn't hike with any cotton clothing and loved the exceptional feeling of cotton sheets in town. Some hostels also have 'hiker clothes' for you to wear while you do

laundry free of charge. Sweat pants and cotton tees... yes please.

- Laundry. Dry out everything (tent, pack, shoes, etc) and wash all of your clothes. There is usually a laundromat in town or a service at the hostel.
- Dump Trash. You will pack out all of your trash from the Trail - food wrappers mainly. Therefore, be sure to throw away anything left over from the recent section. You won't want to accidentally carry it out again on the upcoming leg.
- Shower. The first hot shower when you get to town is the stuff of poetry and miracles. Getting that hiker grime off of you and scrubbing your scalp with shampoo is pure ecstasy.
- Relax. Your body has been crushing miles. Your feet are begging to stay out of your cramped trail shoes. Kick back and enjoy the luxuries of town.
- Resupply. Look at your guide and see how far the next trail town is. Is it 50 miles or 100 miles? Get a rough idea for you daily mileage and plan your food volume accordingly.
- Family and Friends. Call your loved ones and let them know how you are doing. They are going to be curious. Check Facebook, email and all that good stuff if you fancy.
- Dishes. You are not doing the most thorough washing while you are on the Trail. Give your cup, spork and water containers a good hot, soapy wash every time you go to town. I usually did this in hotel sinks or showers with hand soap.
- Charge Electronics. Admittedly, I actually hiked with four electronic devices; flip phone, camera, ebook and iPod. They need to be charged from time to time.

- Other. Order replacement gear, pay bills, etc.

Trail Games.

Stinky Pinky.
My favorite trail game. How it works:
I pick a pair of unrelated words that rhyme and you try to guess what they are based on a pair of synonymous or related 'hint' words I provide you with.

Example 1: (in my Head) I pick "fat rat". I might pick "chubby" as the synonym for "fat" and might pick "varmin" as the synonym for "rat". Therefore, my hint words for you: "chubby varmin". Okay, that was super easy.

Example 2: If I pick "mountain fountain", your hint words could be "hill water" or "summit geyser".

Let's try one now… your hint words: "trouser boogie"

You can get as complicated and as creative as you want. After days of this, we started going to three word rhymes and could hike for hours guessing what the answer could be. Sometimes our guesses were better than the original pick was. I remember waking up the middle of the night in shelters thinking about what my next Stinky Pinky would be. Oh yea, the answer was "pants dance".

Quizzes.
There are endless quizzes to think of. We spent an entire day trying to think of all the state capitals. I had learned them in like 3rd grade and simply forgotten or mixed

some up. Hint: Montpelier is Vermont's capital. Pittsburgh nor Philadelphia are Pennsylvania's capital.

Would You Rather.
I think of two unrelated situations and you, hypothetically, decide which you would prefer to happen. Example: Would you rather be stranded on an arctic island with Michael Jackson or eat tuna for the rest of your life?

Memory Games.
"I went on a hike and brought an (A) Apple."
Next person. "I went on a hike and brought an apple and a (B) Bazooka."
Next person. "I went on a hike and brought an apple, a bazooka and a (C) Carnivorous toy poodle."
Next person. "I went on a hike and brought an apple, a bazooka, a carnivorous toy poodle and a (D) Didgeridoo."
You get the idea.

20 Questions.
I think of something for you to guess and provide you with the category. You have 20 yes-or-no questions to figure it out. If I pick "Michael Jackson", your first question might be "is it a male?" and sometime before question 20 you should be asking "did he wear a white glove and sing Thriller?"

Name that Tune.
I think of a song and say the lyrics in monotone. If you can't guess it, I may sing it.

Storytelling.
Tell your most embarrassing moments, your most scared

moments, etc. This was a great way to get to know other hikers as well as open up to new people.

What are you Going to Eat in Town?

Describe every little detail of that savory burger. Are you going to have one or three pickles? Premix the ketchup and mustard? Or maybe squeeze them both into separate containers and alternate dipping each bite? *Warning*: this game can be dangerous.

Hide Balto.

Find certain trail objects or trinkets and hide them in each other's packs. We found a VHS copy of the animated movie, Balto, in a shelter one day (no idea). We got as creative as possible trying to hide it in each other's packs for weeks. The rule was - if you get caught trying to hide it in someone's pack, you carry it for at least 24 hours. The methods of distraction became rather ornate to say the least. Last I heard, someone had snuck Balto into a NOBO's pack and it, ultimately, made its way to Katahdin. There was also a Beatles biography that I snuck into my friends pack and was not discovered until months after he got off trail. 2 pts.

Charades.

I act out a person, place, phrase, scene, anything. I cannot use props or speak; only my body and hand gestures. You try to guess what I am acting out.

Partying.

Drinking.

Just like the real world, you will find drinkers and nondrinkers. The AT is generally not a party place. Alcohol, particularly beer, is just too heavy to pack. Boozing does not sound particularly appealing either after an exhausting day of hiking. Hiking with a hangover and trying to rehydrate all day... no thanks. If you are big drinker and want to cut loose, town will be your best bet. Most trail towns have at least a bar or liquor store.

Drugs.
I'd be lying if I said you won't encounter marijuana. If the idea of being exposed to marijuana scares you, don't worry. It is not an integral part of the hiking culture and most smoking hikers keep it to themselves and are pretty respectful about where they do it. I did not see any thru-hikers doing anything harder than marijuana on the Trail - no cocaine, heroin, etc.

Tobacco.
Despite being such a physically demanding endeavor, the Trail has a lot of smokers. Probably more than in the real world. Again though, hikers are generally very respectful bunch and won't be obnoxious if it's not your thing.

CHAPTER 6

Trail Life

Shelters.

What are the AT shelters?
Shelters are located *about* every 10 miles along the AT.
Generally, they are three walled wooden structures
elevated a couple feet off the ground. They have a slanted
roof, but are usually tall enough to completely stand up
inside. Inside the shelter is very basic. It is like a big box -
the interior very sparse with maybe one shelf containing
the log book and pen and maybe a broom is tucked away
in the corner to sweep out dirt.

Some have segmented sleeping bunks. Most have just a
wooden floor for you to set up on. Depending on the size,
shelters can sleep anywhere from 6-12 people.

No electricity. Most have a picnic table outside to cook on,
write in your journal, play cards, layout clothes, etc. There
is also usually a fire pit, a water source nearby and a privy.
Privies are trail outhouses located about 50 yards from the
shelter.

Should I sleep in the shelters or my tent?
Long story short, both. Most hikers try to sleep in the shelters as much as possible though.

AT Shelter Pros.
- No Rain. If it rains during the night, you won't have to pack up a wet tent the next morning. Packing up while it is actually raining is even worse. Everything gets wet.
- Space. You can stand up. That is a huge luxury. Your tent can be a tiny, claustrophobic space to change clothes and pack up. If the weather is bad for a long period of time, your tent can turn into a miserable coffin.
- Social. People congregate by the shelters. It is where they sleep and hang out. Half of the fun on the AT is meeting good people.
- Easy. No setting up your tent at night AND no packing it up in the morning.
- Amenities. As mentioned, there is usually water, picnic table and a 'bathroom'.

AT Shelter Cons.
- Inflexible Location. The structures are obviously permanent. Therefore, your hiking mileage revolves around their location. Let's say you wake up sluggish and only feel like hiking 10 miles. You are probably limited to two options - a shelter 5 miles away and then one 20 miles away. You could also encounter nasty weather and need to set up pronto way before reaching the shelter. What if you cross over a beautiful mountain with a nice perch and want to camp out there?
- Crowding. Even as a SOBO, I encountered a few

packed out shelters. NOBO overcrowding is very common and can be a real problem. As my SOBO bubble collided with the NOBO bubble, it was not uncommon for a 10 man shelter to have 20 thru-hikers show up at night. The later half would need to sleep in their tents or hammocks.

- Extra Miles. Sometimes shelters are located half a mile off trail. You might rather set up camp than hike the extra half mile each way.

I slept in the shelters probably 80% of the time and in my tent the other 20%. I HIGHLY recommend bringing your own shelter as a backup option (tent, hammock, tarp, bivy). The AT shelters are a great Plan A, but due to their inflexible location and potential for overcrowding, you want your own Plan B.

Shelter Etiquette.
- First come, first serve. If the weather is bad, make room. You can always put someone at your feet or squeeze in a little bit more. Be considerate before sprawling out all of your gear and becoming a shelter hog.
- Sleeping. Most hikers sleep with the sun. Therefore, 'hiker midnight' is early, just after the sun goes down. Some people snore like gods of thunder so bring ear plugs.
- Cooking. For fear of burning down the wooden shelter, you are not supposed to cook in the shelter. I'll admit that on some cold nights, I did not want to leave my sleeping bag and cooked inside. Be careful if you do.
- Clean. Your crumbs can attract all sorts of wildlife and be a major pain for the next hiker.

Mice.

Extremely common in shelters. A lot of people have slept in the shelters before you and, unfortunately, have trained the mice to know food opportunities await. There are mouse lines to hang your food from inside. These are strings hung from the shelter rafters and have some sort of 'stopper' or block midline to prevent a mouse from crawling down and accessing your hanging food bag.

There were times I went hundreds of miles without seeing or even hearing a mouse. In the most overrun shelters though, mice scurried across my sleeping bag at night and chewed so loud in the corners, I could hardly sleep.

I hung my prized rain shell on a nail one night in the shelter to dry out. The next morning I realized there was a hole big enough for my finger to poke through in the left chest pocket. I had forgotten about an empty granola bar wrapper in there. A mouse had somehow smelled the crumbs, climbed up the wall, and gnawed through my pocket. Lesson learned; hang EVERYTHING edible on the mouse lines. Other than that one incident, the only 'break ins' occurred when I left my food bag on the floor unattended.

Daily Routine.

Everyone is different. Some people get up before sunrise and log big miles. Others sleep in and leisurely start their day mid-morning. I'm somewhere in the middle of those. Here is what a typical day on the trail looked like for me:

8:00 AM Wake up. Eat cold breakfast. Drink a liter of water. Look over my guide and plan that night's destination.

8:30 AM Brush teeth, quick dish rinse, pack up gear, change clothes, stretch.

9:00 AM Hike 4 miles.

10:30 AM Eat a snack and drink my other liter of water.

10:45 AM Hike 4 miles.

12:30 PM Eat lunch at a shelter. Fill up two liters of dirty water and filter both of them. Drink one liter and pack up the other. Check the logbook for any people ahead and leave my entry as well.

1:30 PM Hike 4 miles.

3:30 PM Eat a snack and drink my other liter of water.

3:45 PM Hike 4 miles.

5:30 PM Reach shelter. Change out of hiking shoes and into camp shoes. Change into camp clothes. Unpack and setup sleeping pad and pillow on the shelter floor.

6:00 PM Fill up three liters of dirty water and filter all three. Drink one. Pack one up for breakfast and another for the first midmorning leg of hiking tomorrow.

6:30 PM Cook a hot dinner and eat.

7:30 PM Hang out with everyone. Check the log book and leave an entry.

9:00 PM Read or Journal.

10:00 PM Sleep 10 hours.

Hygiene.

Without running water, the AT will challenge your personal hygiene habits. The changes are gross to some, liberating to others. Let's go over the common activities where you might be used to relying on running water as well as some general hygiene adjustments.

Showering.
Shower in town and don't stress about being dirty on the Trail. Everyone else is dirty so you won't be "THE stinky person". I think I actually started off with some mini soap sheets that dissolved in water. I quickly realized how impractical, not to mention pointless, bathing on the Trail was. That being said, there are plenty of scattered ponds and rivers that are refreshing to jump into on occasion.

Shaving.
Most women stop shaving their legs and armpits. For men, beards are an AT cultural icon. I loved seeing how my beard grew and experiencing my inner caveman. After a few months though, it became extremely irritating and I had to shave it a few times along the way. Some people's skin actually gets infected underneath the beard.

Deodorant.
You don't need it. It is extra weight and can attract mosquitoes. Embrace your natural body odor. It's not as bad as you think!

Brushing Your Teeth.
You can do this without 'wasting' any water. I would wet my mouth by sloshing around a drink of water, then start brushing with the toothbrush and toothpaste. I would spit out the toothpaste (away from human traffic and water sources) as I brushed. By the time I finished, I would suck and spit the bristles until dry, leaving no toothpaste in my mouth or on the brush. I would thoroughly wash my toothbrush with hot water and soap in every town. Sounds a little barbaric. But, it was efficient.

Washing Your Hands.
The Trail can be dirty and you need to keep your hands clean. I used hand sanitizer relentlessly - after the bathroom, before eating and before filtering water. I wouldn't be surprised if a lot of suspected Giardia cases were actually just caused by unwashed hands.

Washing Your Dishes.
Please do not use soap and get the streams sudsy. Even the 'camp safe' biodegradable soaps are not good for natural water sources. There are actually plenty of ways to avoid washing dishes at all. Hot water was the only thing that went in my pot. For the real dirty foods, like oatmeal, I used the packaging as the dish and would pack 'the dishes' out as trash. Worst case, lick your dishes clean or wipe them down with pine needles or your camp towel. You can wash them properly every week in town.

Foot Care.
I put this with 'hygiene' instead of 'first aid' because managing your feet should be as habitual as brushing your teeth. I aired them out every night and often rubbed hand sanitizer on them to get rid of any potential gunk that might be growing. One of my hiking partners carried a small thing of tea tree oil that worked wonders as well. To help with circulation, I recommend trying to keep them slightly elevated for some duration every day. I often propped my feet as I read before bed.

Bathroom Time.

And hygiene is a great segway into bathroom etiquette on the Trail...

Where should I poop at the shelter?

When you are at the shelter, use the privy. They are small permanent wooden outhouses about the size of a porta-potty. Inside is a hollowed seat leading to a deep hole in the ground. Once you have done your business, toss a handful of mulch or leaves on top to help it compost naturally.

Where should I poop on the Trail?

Away from the actual trail and away from water sources. It is a classic rule of thumb to stay 200 feet (or 100 steps) away from the water source. Be careful how far you get off trail though - just enough to not be seen. Otherwise, you can wander too far and get lost. This was the sad cause of a famous thru-hiker's death in 2013.

What is a cathole?

A man made hole designed to do your business. It should be 6-8 inches deep. Use a nearby rock or stick to dig your hole. Some hikers carry a mini shovel (trowel) to dig the hole. Leave No Trace asks for you to pack out your toilet paper. The Appalachian Trail Conservancy asks for you to at least bury it, if not pack it out. Most hikers bury their waste and toilet paper in the cathole below several inches dirt.

How to poop in the woods?

- Sit on a Branch or Rock. Find a fallen tree, horizontal limb, or stable rock to sit on and hang your butt off the back.
- Grab a Tree. Find a standing tree about as thick as your arm or leg. Face the tree and grab it firmly with both hands about belly button high. Sit back and keep your feet close to the base of the tree.

- Squat or Hover. Enough said.

Peeing.
Again, keep away from water sources and anywhere with human traffic. Otherwise, the woods are yours.

Female Needs.
(Males jump ahead to bottom of pg. 73)

I thought it would be best to ask a female directly about this one. Thankfully, AT (and PCT and AZT!) record holder, Heather 'Anish' Anderson (http://facebook.com/AnishHikes) is kind enough to help you ladies out in this section.

-Heather starts writing here-

First things first, there is nothing about being a woman that should limit your ability to enjoy the backcountry. The risk of vaginal and urinary tract infections can be easily negated. In fact, since you can get these at home too, you probably already know how to avoid them. Secondly, menstruation is no different on trail than off (except you may experience a change in flow, often lighter) and the ways you take care of it are the same as well. Feeling a bit better? Good.

Peeing.
You have a few options here.
- Method 1 is the easiest: simply pull down your pants and squat, just like at home.
- Method 2 is to use a pee funnel. A simple online search will give you quite a few brands. These

take a little practice, but they make it easier to urinate without having to squat and bare your buns. You'll want to rinse it (away from surface water) after every use.

- Method 3 is to learn to pee standing up. This takes practice, but is convenient once you get the hang of it. But, there is a pretty high risk of peeing on yourself while you're still learning, so if that bothers you, stick with method 1 or 2. No matter which one you choose, be sure to pack out your TP and urinate away from water sources and the trail.

Many women also use a pee rag or "peedanna". This is a bandanna (or piece of bandanna) dedicated to replacing TP for urine only. This can be a very sanitary option if you follow a few simple rules and it can save you from packing out a lot of TP. It is important to rinse it regularly (away from water sources), wash it in towns using soap, and let it dry on the outside of your pack between uses. If you are already prone to vaginal or urinary tract infections I don't recommend the pee rag method.

Periods.
Yeah, it's never fun. And it's especially not fun to deal with when you're hiking, but, with a few simple adjustments you'll find that it's not too bad. Many women even experience a lighter flow, or shortened period when backpacking, which is a nice bonus!

Menstrual Cup?
Reusable menstrual cups are very popular amongst long distance hikers. There are many brands on the market, Diva Cup being the most popular. They can take some

getting used to, especially at first so if you think you want to try one on the trail, practice with it for a few months at home. They are contraindicated for women with IUD's, a history of vaginal infections, or very heavy flows.

Tampons vs. Pads.
If you do not opt for a Menstrual Cup, you'll be choosing either a pad or tampon. Whichever one you decide to use you must pack out! This includes applicators. Many women use double ziplocs or foil lined ziplocs to cover the sight and smell. I personally use the Mask-It brand odor-proof pouches. These are easy to use and keep the smell and sight of used products hidden. As for deciding between the two, tampons will likely be more comfortable while hiking, however there is an increased risk of infection due to things just not being quite as clean in the backcountry. If you have a history of infections, use pads instead.

Always clean your hands with soap and water/wet wipes/hand sanitizer before inserting a tampon. Never use an antibacterial wipe or hand sanitizer in or around your V! This kills the good bacteria living on your skin which actually helps keep you from getting infections. Use soap and water (or just water) away from a water source or a wet wipe without antibacterial qualities.

-Heather ends writing here -

Magic, Angels and Names.

Trail Magic.
A random act of kindness. Anything from being offered

some Mike and Ike's or being offered a free place to stay. A trail crossing might have a cooler hidden behind a tree with a few cold drinks and a nice note of inspiration. You might come to a trail crossing and have someone with a grill and hot dogs, water, anything. The AT is full of Trail Magic and people doing kind deeds without any expectations.

Some of my favorite Trail Magic:
- A liquor store in Connecticut. At the checkout, a customer heard we were thru-hiking and opened a $100 tab for 6 of us to stock up on.
- A rural dirt road crossing in Tennessee. A nearby church had packed free Bibles and Moon Pies into a nearby cooler with a heartfelt note.
- A lady had been hiking for 8 miles before she found some thru-hikers. She had made hummus and red pepper sandwiches for us.
- Countless people who offered me rides while hitchhiking. Even if it was raining and I stunk to high heaven, many were glad to drive out of their way to get me back to the trailhead or get me into town.
- Countless people who put me up in their house, did my laundry, cooked for me and shuttled me to the trail.
- A Thanksgiving feast in Hot Springs, NC hosted free of charge.

Trail Angels.
Givers of Trail Magic. You will meet some Trail Angel legends. These people dedicate a huge amount of time to taking care of thru-hikers. There were towns, like Hanover, that had lists of trail angels to call for a place to

stay.

Trail Names.
Everyone has one. These become your trail identity and substitute your real name entirely. Most people get their trail name within a week or two of being on the Trail. There is no official naming process - you can even name yourself. Most people get one for something unique they do or say early on. Hilarious and lighthearted or thoughtful and meaningful, every trail name has a story.

A few examples of how some people get their trail name:

- Smooth (me): I had just gotten back from a three month bicycle tour of New Zealand and, similar to the AT, did not have frequent access to showers. Therefore, I shaved my legs to make it easy to just wipe myself down (don't judge!). A few nights into the AT, someone asked why I shaved my legs and I instantly became "Smooth". Note this often made me sound like a self-proclaimed ladies' man and, subsequently, a huge douche bag. If I were to do it again, I would make my own trail name. "Cowabunga" from Teenage Mutant Ninja Turtles and "Rufio" from Hook are leading contenders.
- Shutterbug: She carried around a big camera and took a lot of pictures.
- Forever Sunrise: One of the most optimistic people I have ever met.
- Hover Job: He went into an in depth description of his method of using the public facilities.
- Other Names I hiked with: *2 Liter, Ado, Afternoon Delight, Bartender, Bearbait, Big Dog, Blondie, Blue Sky, Bluetick, Bojangles, Boss, Breeze, Buck, Bugaboo, Buzz, Cerveza, Chaco, Chalupa, Chef, Chef Beard,*

Chewy, Chicory, Chimp, Cocoa, Commissary,
Cowshead, Crunchmaster, Delta, De Jesus, Doctor
Scholls, Dog Whisperer, Echo, El Flaco, EZ-Rock,
Fartmaster, Fireball, Fives, Flip, Freaky John, Friar
Bob, Funk, Furprittius, Glamis, Globe, Goatman,
Google, Gospel, Gramps, Groucho, Happy Ending,
Harpo, Honkey, Ice Pack, Jubilee, Junco, Kosmonaught,
Leg-it, Magnet, Mapless, Maverick, McLovin,
Milkrun, Moto!, Mutts Butts, Nectar, Ninja, One
Verse, Our Manager, Pabst, Patches, Phoenix,
Pineapple, Pivot, Pockets, Polechar, Potato Shake,
Potter, PT, Pumba, Rebar, Rock Lobster, Rope, Rooster,
Shelob, Sherpa, Shuffle, Skunk, Skurks, Slips, Smash,
So Heavy, Sourpatch, Spits, Sprout, Stilts, Stinky
Jesus, Streamwalker, Stub, Sumo, Taxi, The Captain,
The Governor, Trashcan, Turducken, Treegasm, Tsu
La, Up, Wildcat, Wolfbird, Woodbutcher, Woody, Yea
Yea, Yogi, Ziploc.

Respect the Trail.

The goal is to not leave any impact or trace of your visit -
referred to as "leave no trace". There is also an
organization of the same name echoing a similar message.
Use this as a framework for minimizing your outdoor
footprint. The basics…

- Everything should stay 'as is'. Don't chop down
  trees, break off branches, dig deep trenches, block
  streams, build structures, etc.
- Keep fires in existing fire rings. Make sure the fire
  is completely out before leaving it. This also
  means try to camp at existing campsites, instead of
  creating your own.

- Leave wildlife alone. Only observe. Don't feed them, handle them, etc.
- Bury human waste properly.
- Pack out trash and dispose of in town.

Dogs.

I hiked a section of Pennsylvania with three people who, collectively, were hiking with two dogs. We had seen a few warnings posted on trees about the dense porcupine population and paid no attention. Sure enough, one of the dogs picked up a scent and wandered off trail to explore. The unsuspecting porcupine skewered one of the dog's snout with a handful of sharp 6 inch quills. In addition to the dog's pain and suffering, all three hikers had to get off trail for several days and find a ride to the nearest veterinarian.

If you have a dog, I'm sure you have thought about the possibilities of throwing a saddle pack on them and testing their trail legs. You might not be able to find someone who can take care of him for 6 months anyway. They're animals and made for this kind of outdoor hiking stuff, right? Maybe.

Thru-hiking the AT can certainly be done with a dog. A few considerations though:
- Temperament. Hiking with a dog on a leash will be impractical. He will need to be well trained and not run off to attack a bear or even, another dog or human. As mentioned, porcupines are a very common problem in a few sections. I never knew any dogs that were bitten by snakes. However, I

imagine that could be a big problem considering how often I saw them.

- Hair. Dogs cannot 'layer' their clothes with the weather. A heavy fur coat can be comfortable in winter, but torturous in summer. If your dog has a thick coat, I'd recommend shaving him and bringing sweaters as needed.
- Ability. Is he an athletic breed able to walk long miles every day? Is he young without any health conditions? Your dog should be able to carry a lot of his own weight - his own food, water, etc. My black lab came hiking with me once and she could barely keep up. Therefore, she would need some serious training. Otherwise, she would be dead weight on the AT. Sorry Stella.

Pros of Hiking with a Dog.
- Fun. I loved arriving at the shelter at night and having dogs to play with.
- Companion. Another guy I hiked with became best friends with his dog. He talked about how hiking with his dog was one of the best decisions he made.
- Safety. A dog can certainly provide a sense of comfort from wildlife and, potentially, other humans.

Cons of Hiking with a Dog.
- Extra Work. Feeding, resupplying, watering, paw maintenance, changing clothes, bathing, pooping, etc.
- Less Wildlife. After hiking with a dog for a few days, I realized how little wildlife I was seeing. The dogs tended to wander ahead and, I assumed,

alert all wildlife we were coming.

- No Pets Allowed. Many hostels and hotels won't allow pets at all. Hitchhiking could be an extra challenge. Two sections (Smoky Mountain and Baxter State Park) do not allow dogs on the Trail forcing you to board them.

Dog Gear List.
- Dog Boots. Your dog's feet will need to be protected.
- Pack. Saddlebags on each side. Name tag identification as well.
- Leash for town and congested parts of the trail.
- Tick Kit or Bug Spray. They will wander through grass and be more likely to gather ticks than you.
- Light Clip. You want to be able to see them at night.
- Consumables. Dehydrated food and water. You should research this on your own depending on your dog's needs.

Electronics.

Whether or not you should pack electronics is a big debate. Some feel you should embrace the simple life and reject society's fast-pace technology. Others feel that it can make things easier, safer and enhance the overall experience.

Chargers.
Assuming you decide to bring a few electronics, the biggest problem is keeping them charged. Few items can last a week without charge. I do not recommend solar

chargers either. There is no consistent sunshine in the woods to charge them. They are also heavy, bulky and can be a pain to setup. You will need to charge everything in town.

Cameras.

I carried a weatherproof camera. My AT photos are extremely valuable to me now and I am so grateful I prioritized taking photos. You need something that can drop on a rock or in a pond. Cell phone cameras are so good now though, I might vote to consolidate the flip phone and the camera for a 'rough' smartphone. A thick case could help ensure its protection.

eBook.

Few people carry ebooks. Too heavy to pack, too tired to read, not interested, who knows. As mentioned, my Kindle was a lifesaver, especially on rainy days. I could read part of an adventure tale and switch over to a field guide. It was super light and had a battery that lasted several weeks. I made a DIY cover out of a sock and some cardboard.

Phone Reception.

Most places on the AT are very remote and do not have reception. I brought a flip phone and kept it turned off while on the Trail. I turned it on in town and only used it to call my family or book a hostel. And, of course, it was available in case of an emergency. Anything fancier than a flip phone though and I'd be worried about crushing it or getting it wet.

The first week on the Trail, I remember subconsciously reaching for my phone in my pocket to check any recent notifications. It felt great realizing my phone was not there. For years, I had developed a habitual and subconscious 'phone check'. It felt like I had been eerily trained and I loved breaking that habit.

WIFI.
Most hostels and hotels have free WIFI. Some have computers to use. Otherwise, many restaurants or libraries in town will have access.

Social Media and Blogging.
If you are a big social media person, awesome. I'm sure your Facebook friends will enjoy following your journey. I am not super comfortable sharing every detail of my life on social media though. I found trailjournals.com a more comfortable way to post my updates publicly. Family and friends could visit my page on the site and read my most recent entry and see my most recent photos when they wanted. There is a big community already on Trail Journals that may enjoy following along as well.

Money.

Other than a few exceptions, there is nowhere *on* the Trail to buy anything. Carrying cash should really only be needed for emergencies. Since you will go through a trail town every few days or, a week at most, you will frequently have access to an ATM.

I carried about $50 cash at a time along with a debit card. A debit card, not credit card, because I did not want to deal with the bill payments. I would always try to pay with a debit card. The $50 cash would be enough to get me through if they did not accept plastic - the first night at a hostel, to catch a bus or taxi if I had an accident, buy lunch if there was a small shop at a trail crossing, etc.

CHAPTER 7

Meet the AT

Simply known as 'The A.T.', the Appalachian Trail is an iconic continuous footpath stretching 2,185 miles along the Appalachian Mountains on the east coast of the United States. It starts at the Southern Terminus on Springer Mountain, Georgia and ends at the Northern Terminus on Mt. Katahdin, Maine. The Trail traverses through 6 National Parks and 14 states - Georgia, North Carolina, Tennessee, Virginia, West Virginia, Maryland, Pennsylvania, New Jersey, New York, Connecticut, Massachusetts, Vermont, New Hampshire, and Maine.

The Appalachian Mountains are considered to be one of the oldest mountain ranges in the world. They formed an estimated one billion years ago and are thought to have reached 15,000 feet, rivaling the present day Rockies. They have slowly been eroding since then into what they are today. The highest point is at 6,643 feet on top of Clingman's Dome in North Carolina and the lowest point is at 124 feet at Bear Mountain State Park in New York.

There are dozens of subranges of the Appalachian Mountain Range. The Allegheny Mountains, The White

Mountains, The Blue Ridge Mountains, Green Mountains, The Great Smoky Mountains and The Catskills to name a few.

From 107 degree record highs in the Southern summer days to -47 degree record lows on Mt. Washington, the temperature can range in over 150 degrees Fahrenheit. Mt. Washington, NH also holds 2nd place for the fastest winds ever recorded on earth. At 231 miles an hour, it still holds the record for fastest winds not associated with a tropical cyclone.

The concept of the AT is credited to Benton MacKaye in 1921 and completed later, thanks to the help of Myron Avery, in 1937. MacKaye is often credited as the 'dreamer' and Avery as the 'doer'. The two never spoke again after a bitter rivalry over the development of Skyline Drive in Shenandoah National Park.

The Appalachian Trail is considered the largest and longest running volunteer conservation project in the world. Some 33 organizations and 4,000 volunteers hit the Trail every year to ensure the trails are safe and clean.

The AT has become hugely popular in pop culture. Books (and movies) like <u>A Walk in the Woods</u> have brought the trail experience to a mass audience. This popularity has spawned new long distance trails like the Continental Divide Trail (NM, CO, WY, ID, MT) and the Pacific Crest Trail (CA, OR, WA).

Anyone who completes the entire Trail within one-year is considered to be a "thru-hiker". A thru-hike usually takes anywhere from 4-7 months to complete... 5.5 months being the average.

The Appalachian Trail Conservancy estimates 1,000 - 2,000 hikers attempt to thru-hike the Trail every. Since the Trail's completion, less than 15,000 people have actually thru-hiked the AT.

While Myron Avery was the first to completely hike the length of the Trail, Earl Schaffer was the first to complete a thru-hike in 1948. The first woman to thru-hike it was 'Grandma Gatewood'. She completed it at 67 years old! There have been countless other notable thru-hikers - from people with amputated limbs to people carrying tubas and plastic pink flamingos. Bill Irwin was a famous blind thru-hiker who took 8 months to complete the Trail with thousands of falls and several cracked ribs.

Many people have been attempting to break the record to complete the 2,185 miles long trail - known as the 'FKT' or 'Fastest Known Time'. There are two ways to attempt the FKT 1) unsupported: carry all personal gear and camp just like any other thru-hiker or 2) supported: typically having a team in a van carry supplies and having a bed to sleep in at night. As expected, the supported record is faster than the unsupported.

As of this writing, the FKT supported record is held by Karl 'The Goat' Meltzer for completing the Trail in 43 days and 9 hours and 6 minutes (about 50 miles per day). The FKT unsupported record is held by Heather 'Anish' Anderson at 47 days and 10 hours and 2 minutes (about 46 miles per day). That's nearly 2 marathons a day, *every day*. Insane.

CHAPTER 8

State By State Breakdown

Let's get one thing out of the way - there are no 'easy' sections of the Appalachian Trail. After all, this is a mountain range with countless ups and downs (pun intended). The AMC estimates over 500,000 feet of elevation change. This change is substantially more than the Continental Divide Trail and nearly double the amount on the Pacific Crest Trail.

To clarify, a typical hiking trail might start at 5,000 feet in elevation and climb up to 7,000 feet over a span of 5 miles... a total elevation change of *2,000 feet*. For a similar 5 mile stretch, the AT might start at 2,000 feet in elevation and go up to 3,000, then down to 1,500, then up to 3,000 again... a total elevation change of *4,000 feet*.

In short, the AT is REALLY hilly.

In addition to massive amounts of elevation change, the AT's trail itself is known for being very 'gnarly'. By 'gnarly', I mean containing lots of roots and stumps and rocks and twists and turns and things that have the potential to make you stumble. This 'gnarly factor' can significantly slow down your pace because it demands you pay much closer attention to each and every foot placement.

That being said, we can compare each section relative to one another. A few questions we can ask to judge the difficulty of the trail are:

1) Are there switchbacks?
Switchbacks are trail luxuries that essentially break up how steep an incline is. Instead of hiking straight up a mountain, switchbacks zig-zag the trail up the mountain for an easier graded ascent. It's the same principle as a wheelchair ramp - we'd rather push grandma up a slow and steady ramp instead of a short and steep ramp, right?

2) Is it wet?
Some sections have swampy bogs or flooding rivers that take a big toll on your feet as well as your pace.

3) Is it rocky?
Some sections are riddled with ankle twisting rocks. A couple have big boulders that require you to get on all fours and scramble over. Some rocks make it feel like you are climbing a stair case - except each stair step is three feet high.

I am not going to focus too much on weather simply because everyone hikes at different times of the year. Let's shed some light on each state now.

Georgia.

Length: 78.5 miles (0 to 78.5)

Highest Point: 4,458 ft. (Blood Mountain)

Overview and Why it is Awesome:
Springer Mountain has become an iconic landmark for the Appalachian Trail. This is where it all begins (or ends). Blood Mountain is the first big mountain for Northbounders. It has stunning panoramic views of the surrounding mountains. A historic stone shelter, built in 1934 by the CCC (Civilian Conservation Corps), is perched on the summit.

Mountain Crossings Outfitters at Neels Gap is the first real hostel and outfitter you will reach. It is also the only man made structure the AT goes through. A tree full of hanging hiker boots stands as a marker for all of those who have come before. Most thru-hikers go through what is called a 'shakedown' here. The employees at Mountain Crossings are seasoned hikers and can provide a lot of gear advice, help lighten your load and ship home any unwanted stuff.

Despite being the warmest state the AT goes through, Georgia is often the coldest section for most thru-hikers. It can still snow in March in North Georgia when the big bubble of Nourthbounders sets off. This harsh weather at the start can be a tough test for any wary hikers. Southbounders finishing in Georgia in November have been known to encounter heavy snow storms as well (I did!).

As far as terrain, Georgia is a fairly easy to moderate section of the AT. The Trail is well marked and well maintained. There are not any bogs, swamps or heavy rocky areas either. Keep in mind there is plenty of elevation change though.

North Carolina/ Tennessee.

Length: 386.7 miles (78.5 to 465.1)

Highest Point: 6,643 ft. (Clingman's Dome)

Overview and Why it's Awesome:
North Carolina and Tennessee are listed as 'one state' here because the Trail snakes in and out along their border making it hard to differentiate the two.

When I think of North Carolina and Tennessee, I think of wild flowers, flowing streams, spruce-fir forest, and grassy balds. This is generally a favorite state(s) for thru-hikers... myself included.

There are two record-high elevation landmarks in this section; Roan High Knob Shelter and Clingman's Dome. At 6,285 ft, Roan High Knob Shelter is the highest shelter on the AT. At 6,643 ft., Clingman's Dome is the highest point on the AT.

'The Smokys'. The Trail goes through 70 miles of the Great Smoky Mountains. This section contains the largest old growth forest and the densest population of black bears in the East. 'Old growth' means forest that has been relatively undisturbed by man (logging, etc.). These trees are massive and feel prehistoric. I had no idea how little old growth actually remained in the USA until I hiked through this section. The spruce-fir forest is simply majestic.

There are several famous grassy balds like Hump Mountain and Max Patch here as well. Roan Highlands is a small section that contains the longest stretch of grassy bald on the entire Trail. The Trail goes along an elevated, open, grassy ridge line with amazing views.

Hot Springs, NC is one of the most popular trail towns. It is a historic and charming town with fewer than 1,000 citizens. You can walk down the main street to French Broad River or to one of the only natural hot springs in the entire Southeast.

Virginia.

Length: 540.6 miles (465.1 to 1,005.7)

Highest Point: 5,729 ft. (Mt. Rogers down a short side trail)

Overview and Why it's Awesome:
This state is massive. It makes up 25% of the entire trail length. Many people get what are known as the "Virginia Blues" because it feels so endless.

Damascus is one of the most well-known trail towns for its famous festival, Trail Days. Most Northbounders bottle neck into Damascus for the festival in mid-May.

Wood's Hole hostel was one of my favorite hostels. Set half a mile off trail, this log cabin and 100 acre farm was built in the 1880's. The owners make some great homemade meals.

A group of ponies was introduced to Grayson Highlands State Park several hundred years ago. Since then, they have grown to a herd over 100 strong and freely graze the grasslands. In addition to ponies, the Grayson Highlands section offers long, flat trails with big views at 5,000 ft. above sea level.

McAfee Knob is the 'most photographed spot' on the Appalachian Trail. This emblematic rock jets out like Pride Rock from *The Lion King* and is the cover of the movie, *A Walk in the Woods*. The Trail continues to follow the beautiful limestone ledge into Tinker Cliffs and provides even more views.

The Shenandoahs, or 'Shenny's', is a 75 mile long subrange of the Appalachian Mountains located in central Virginia. The high concentration of black bears and beautiful overlooks make it a popular and more touristy section (Shenandoah National Park) of the Trail.

Virginia is known for quality trail with gradual climbs. It is not flat by any means. There are plenty of big climbs as well as the 'roller coaster' section. But, because it has less elevation than some other states, it is often thought of as flat in comparison.

West Virginia.

Length: 17.7 miles (1,005.7 to 1,023.4)

Highest Point: 1,650 ft.

Overview and Why it's Awesome:
This section is tiny and can be covered in a day. The main attraction in West Virginia is the historic town, Harper's Ferry. While not exactly halfway, it is considered the 'halfway hub'. Meaning this is the largest town near the halfway point. Most hikers use this point to flip-flop north or south from.

The Appalachian Trail Conservancy is headquartered here and will take your photograph to be placed in the hiker archives. These books document decade's worth of thousands of hikers. This is as official as it gets for your thru-hiker award and recognition status.

The town is situated at the confluence of the historical Shenandoah River and Potomac River. I recommend reading Midnight Rising before you reach Harper's Ferry. It tells the tale of the famous raid on Harper's Ferry by the abolitionist John Brown.

Maryland.

Length: 40.6 miles (1,023.4 to 1,064)

Highest Point: 1,795 ft.

Overview and Why it's Awesome:
I wish I had something awesome to say about Maryland. There was nothing bad about it, but nothing too noteworthy either. You also cross a 'Mason-Dixon Line' marker from Maryland into Pennsylvania and a nice overlook at Washington Monument.

Pennsylvania.

Length: 229.3 miles (1,064 to 1,293.3)

Highest Point: 2,040 ft.

Overview and Why it's Awesome:
Pennsylvania is one of the flattest states. But, rocks, rocks, rocks. Maybe some more rocks after that. The rocks are often about the size of basketballs and notorious for turning ankles. The constant angling of ankles can be extremely frustrating on long days when you just want to WALK and not tip toe or calculate every hop.

Pennsylvania destroys shoes and will test your rattlesnake spotting ability. Out of only a handful of rattlesnake sightings, most of mine were in Pennsylvania.

The Doyle Hotel is a must stop. This place has character. Originally built in the late 1700's and rebuilt after a fire in the early 1900's, it hosted many famous residents like Charles Dickens. It has inexpensive rooms and a great second floor balcony to chomp down on a burger and enjoy cold beer.

A few more random notes. There seemed to be a lot of

'Chicken of the Woods' growing in Pennsylvania which is an edible mushroom that grows in huge orange patches on wet logs and trees. I saw several groups of Amish hiking and a horse and carriage at a road crossing as well. The Pinnacle is a big climb with a great view.

New Jersey.

Length: 72.1 miles (1,293.3 to 1,365.4)

Highest Point: 1,653 ft. (Sunrise Mountain)

Overview and Why it's Awesome:
A lot more wildlife than expected. Expect several bear sightings and a beautiful wildlife sanctuary. The Trail wraps around the perimeter of the grassy sanctuary. I saw several bald eagles flying, nesting and feeding. Sunfish Pond is beautiful - a pristine and glass-like body of water engulfed by rich forest. There is a massive 1.5 mile wooden boardwalk in New Jersey that is great for an easy stroll.

New York.

Length: 92.6 miles to (1,365.4 to 1,458)
*Note the trail overlaps in and out of CT and NY here.

Highest Point: 1,433 ft. (Prospect Rock)

Overview and Why it's Awesome:
You are able to see the New York City skyline off in the distance for a small section. There is even a railroad station on the Trail that takes you directly into Grand Central

Station. A two hour ride and you can go see The Big Apple. Just be aware of your smell. Most subway passengers were not pleased with my hygiene. Lifting up my arms to hold on to the handles was like activating a six-foot impenetrable force field.

You will cross over the famous Hudson River and pass West Point Academy where Dwight D. Eisenhower, Robert E. Lee, George S. Patton and a boatload of other notable military leaders graduated. Just after the bridge is a 'trail zoo' that hosts rescued animals. Black bears, coyotes, owls, snakes and a wide variety of other animals from the area are there. Just next door is a trail museum.

A few more notes... New York has the biggest tree on the entire Trail. No hitchhiking in New York. Probably the most most crowded section for hiking. Bear Mountain was particularly congested. Bear Mountain, at 124 ft, is also the lowest point on the Trail.

Connecticut.

Length: 47.8 miles (1,458 to 1505.8)

Highest Point: 2,316 ft. (Bear Mountain; different one from NY)

Overview and Why it's Awesome:
Similar to West Virginia and Maryland, this section is small. Still pretty, but not much noteworthy. No campfires are permitted. Bulls Bridge was a highlight. There is a rope swing and a small convenience store nearby. My hiking crew and I sprawled out eating junk food and swinging

into the river for hours.

Massachusetts.

Length: 90.5 miles (1,505.8 to 1,596.3)

Highest Point: 3,491 ft. (Mt. Greylock)

Overview and Why it's Awesome:
Mt. Greylock is a landmark. You can see five states from its summit and many famous people have reached it. The author of <u>Moby Dick</u>, Herman Melville, is said to have gotten inspiration for the big whale from this humped mountain. Mt. Everett is another beauty full of old growth pitch pine and scrub oak.

Upper Goose Pond was a favorite shelter. It is actually more of a private cabin than a shelter. It is .5 miles off trail and nestled on the edge of a beautiful pond. You can take the canoes out, go for a swim and get some sun. We canoed to the other end of the pond and ordered some pizza to a parking lot and canoed back at sunset. The next morning, some caretakers made us all-you-can-eat pancakes for free. Hallelujah!

Some parts of Massachusetts are congested. Not by foot traffic, but by houses. You will walk through several backyards and a few neighborhoods.

Vermont.

Length: 150.1 miles (1,596.3 to 1,746.4)

Highest Point: 3,908 ft. (Cooper Lodge Shelter/ Killington Peak)

Overview and Why it's Awesome:
This was my favorite section of the Trail. I remember having a lot of fun in Vermont and, for the first time, really enjoying the Appalachian Trail as a lifestyle (remember, I was SOBO). Vermont does not have the most dramatic mountains or breathtaking overlooks. It does not have any iconic AT landmarks or particularly unique wildlife either. To me, though, Vermont just felt peaceful.

The Trail is much more moderate which was a huge relief from the relentlessly harsh climbs in Maine and New Hampshire. Also, I had developed what are referred to as my 'trail legs'. This is when your legs are in shape for hiking. The aches and pains are never ending throughout the hike for most people. However, they are much worse at the beginning of the Trail and become more subtle once you get your sturdy trail legs.

In late July, everything is a lush green. Many parts have wild flowers and thick grasses hugging the dirt footpath. Wild blueberry patches are a daily encounter.

The SOBO bubble (if there ever was one) had thinned out and I was hiking with some great folks.

One of my favorite nights was on top of Mt. Bromley. It is used for skiing in winter and has wide mowed down sections leftover from the routes in summer. There is a gondola perched on top and a small hut that is open for thru-hikers to sleep in. Three of us watched the sunset from the gondola. The stars were bright that night and we

stayed up for hours watching them by the fire.
Stratton Mountain is where James P. Taylor conceived
'The Long Trail' (another long-distance trail) and also
where Benton Mackaye conceived the Appalachian Trail.
There is a small fire tower on top for a better view.

New Hampshire.

Length: 160.9 miles (1,746.4 to 1,907.3)

Highest Point: 6,288 ft. (Mt. Washington)

Overview and Why it's Awesome:
New Hampshire contains some of the most dramatic
landscape - big mountains and epic overlooks. It has the
largest amount of above-treeline-trail than any other state.
This is considered to be the toughest state. The trail is
poorly graded and often without switchbacks making the
climbs much more taxing on your body.

The Presidential Range is a subrange of The White
Mountains and contains the highest mountains in the
Northeast. As mentioned, Mt. Washington once held the
world record for wind speeds and continues to be a
potentially dangerous summit (don't forget to moon the
cog railway full of tourists on their way to the summit - an
old thru-hiker tradition). There are a couple of ponds
scattered along the Trail here as well. On a clear day, they
will mirror the sky. Franconia Ridge is another stunning
section just before The Presidential Range.

Hanover, NH is the home of the Dartmouth College and
the Trail goes right through town. There is a strong trail

angel support system here. We enjoyed free food at some restaurants and free places to stay with great hosts.

Maine.

Length: 281.8 miles (1907.3 to 2189.1)

Highest Point: 5,268 ft. (Mt. Katahdin)

Overview and Why it's Awesome:
"No pain, no Maine"... so the trail phrase goes. Maine is a big state and has some rough trail. If New Hampshire is rugged peaks, then Maine is rugged trail. As in wet roots, rocks, moss, and mud everywhere. Every step and foot placement takes a little more consideration in Maine. The Southern states are known for well maintained trail. Not Maine. Similar to New Hampshire, Maine has some unforgiving and steep climbs with minimal (or no) switchbacks.

The Mahoosuc Notch is often called 'the toughest mile' on the AT. This mile stretch is full of massive shelter-size boulders. To get through the boulder field, you will need to set aside your trekking poles and rock scramble. I loved it. It felt good to jump around and duck underneath the rocks.

The 100 Mile Wilderness is a remote wilderness nearly submerged in wetlands. Crossing only a few gravel roads, this is as pristine as it gets on the Appalachian Trail. This is also where you are most likely to spot a moose. There are bogs, waterfalls and rocky river crossings. The 100 Mile Wilderness is the last section for NOBOs just before

Mt. Katahdin.

...and the big beauty herself, Mt. Katahdin. The iconic end of the Trail for Northbounders and the beginning for Southbounders. Henry David Thoreau famously climbed it in the 1800's. The highest mountain in Maine, Mt. Katahdin is a dramatic climb that requires some more boulder scrambling. The summit has one of the best views on the entire Appalachian Trail... and celebration awaits.

For weather and safety concerns, Mt. Katahdin is not available to climb past October 15th.

CHAPTER 9

Gear Guide

Your Life in 40 Items.
These are the only possessions you will have for 6 months.
This gear is going to become a part of you - your trail skin,
your battle armor, your regalia. Your life will boil down to
roughly 40 items. Every item will serve a purpose, ideally
several purposes. You will get to know these items
probably more than any other tangible items in your life.

You will know every curve and contour of your eating
utensil. Like the fluid motion of shifting gears, you will
mindlessly click your headlamp twice and then hold it
down for three seconds (not five!) to activate the red light
setting. By the end of the Trail, you will be able to pack
and unpack your bag blindfolded in record time.

I sometimes found it comical just how quickly I could
setup my tent. I learned which hand to overlap first when
unfolding the tent, whip it so it floated to the ground in
position, effortlessly connect the poles, drive the stakes
down in order, feel the optimal tension of the guylines,
every… little… detail.

The biggest mistake thru-hikers make with their gear is bringing everything they will need... or think they will need for 6 months.

"Sunglasses? Yea, sure. Might be nice to have 'em". Not quite. The might-be-nice-to-have items are only going to weigh you down.

I had a gear rule on the AT; if *you are not using an item every day, you don't need it.* Other than a couple of items in my first aid kit, I used every item in my pack heavily.

Gear hunting is half of the fun when planning your thru-hike and you should enjoy it. You will also inevitably find things that work better for you as you go. Therefore, don't stress about getting the 'perfect' items. If something doesn't work quite right, you can always change it out.

Let's Get Nerdy.
If you are totally green to backpacking, don't let this section overwhelm you. I still had my Boy Scout gear that my parents bought me for my 14th birthday before I started researching thru-hiking gear. The gear has advanced A LOT since 2002. Canvas is out and Cuben Fiber is in. External frames are collecting dust in attics and boots are only for the military and hunting.

The main goal of this chapter is to make sure you understand thru-hiking gear... the options, the pros and cons of each, and hopefully enough information for you to decide what will work for you. It would be better to change out only a handful of your items along the way instead of a complete overhaul. Ya dig?

Let's jump into all of this. Grab a cup of coffee and a highlighter or a note pad.

Why is going lightweight important?
- Reduces Likelihood of Injury. Less weight on your knees, ankles and back.
- Fuel Efficiency. Consider yourself an engine. The lighter your load, the less fuel (food and energy in your case) it takes to get the same distance.
- Comfort. You want to be like a gazelle soaring over mountains, not moaning and groaning up every hill.

Lightweight vs Ultralight.
Thru-hikers already place a big emphasis on keeping things lightweight. Ultralight takes it to the nerd core extreme. Defining what is 'ultralight' vs 'lightweight' can be somewhat loose though as there is no set poundage that acts as a cutoff point.

Ultralight hikers are known to be rather obsessive - weigh every item to the gram and shave any potentially unnecessary gram off, literally. Their gear is often do-it-yourself and made at home or by 'cottage industries'. You won't find many cottage industry products at your local REI. They are usually made out of someone's garage and sold directly from their website. The ultralight obsession over shaving grams has become somewhat of a hobby itself and a subculture within the backpacking community.

Don't Be 'stupid light'.
Sure, ultralight sounds kinda cool, eh? Not many thru-hikers are the obsessive ultralight type though. Simply put, ultralight is often impractical... especially for a long

period of time like a thru-hike. Going ultralight sometimes means 'doing without'.

For example, an ultralight hiker might leave the stove behind and only eat non-cook food or use a razor blade instead of a knife.

Gear selection is clearly a tough balancing act between minimal weight and high utility. I want all of my gear to be high functioning and weigh as light as a feather too. Just don't let your weight sacrifices lead to a miserable or unsafe hike.

Base Weight.
A common question will be "what is your base weight". This is referring to the weight of all of your gear without any consumables (food and water). Thru-hikers should aim to keep their base weight below 20 lbs. With several days of food and a liter of water, that will put you around 30 lbs. total. Ultralight backpackers aim for under a 10 lb. base weight.

Total Pack Weight - Consumables = Base Weight.

Backpack.

By far one of the most important pieces of gear.

Volume.
"If you have it, you will fill it." Meaning if you carry a large pack, you will assume that you have the extra space and will bring more stuff. Carrying a smaller pack can be somewhat advantageous because it forces you to prioritize

your item selection to be lighter and more compact.
I recommend a carrying capacity of no less than 40 liters
and no more than 65 liters. 50 to 55 liters is a good middle
ground. My pack was 58 liters and I would have liked just
a tiny bit less space. 40 liters would be my ideal volume.
I'll admit though that it would be a challenge for me to fit
everything into 40 liters, especially with any extra winter
gear and a full week's worth of food.

Note many manufacturers include the external pockets as
part of their measured carrying capacity. You will pack
items on the outside of your pack - water bottle, rain shell,
etc.

Comfort and Fit.
It needs to feel right. This baby will be on your hips and
shoulders for 8 hours a day... and taken off and put back
on several times a day. The manufacturer should have
some sort of torso measuring method to make sure you get
the right size. You want to securely clip the belt above
your hip bones so the majority of the pack's weight rides
on your hips instead of your shoulders. I often lean
forward a bit and take my arms out of the shoulder straps
to test how comfortable the weight is if entirely on my
hips.

Frames.
In my Boy Scout days, many backpacks had thick,
rectangular, external metal frames. Fortunately, those have
nearly gone extinct and have been replaced by thin
internal metal frames that outline the contours of your
body. Many packs use plastic sheets or foam pads or no
frames at all. As gear becomes lighter and lighter, the need
for a stable and supportive frame is becoming less and

less. The importance of the frame or back panel has shifted to an emphasis more on breathability instead of support. Many packs have a concave back panel to maximize airflow. While helpful, take this 'airflow' with a grain of salt. Even with one of the most breathable packs on the market, I was still a sweaty pig most days. The biggest use I found for the back panel cushion or concave frame was preventing items in my pack from jabbing into my back.

Compartments and Pockets.
You want your gear as accessible as possible without any unnecessary bells and whistles.

- Hip Pockets. The pockets on the hip belt. I loved having these. Stuffing a snack or camera or knife in these pockets was so convenient. I did not like anything weighing down my pant or short pockets. And, when wearing running shorts, I didn't even have pockets, making the hip belt pockets that much more necessary.
- Main Cavity. The main storage area. I like having one big internal compartment. Some packs have built-in 'shelves' that are inflexible and add weight.
- Side Pockets. 2 thumbs up for these. Nice to be able to easily access your water bottle while hiking.
- Brain. This is the 'head flap' on the top of some packs. Provides quick access to small gear items that may not fit into the hip pockets. Sometimes it is removable and can be used as a day pack. I find them too floppy and frankly, unnecessary.
- Water Bladder. A small slip tucked against your back inside the main compartment. If you plan on using a water bladder with a hose, this sleeve

would be helpful to keep your bladder vertical. Keeping it vertical will let gravity do its job to settle the water at the bottom of the bladder and drink every last drop.

- Mesh Front. I like for this pocket to be big and airy. Use it to put your camp shoes in or dry out a stinky piece of clothing. I highly recommend getting a pack with one.
- Shoulder Pocket. I kept my hand sanitizer here tied to a 6 inch piece of twine - just like a pen attached to the bank counter. This pocket is not necessary at all. But, I probably stayed a bit cleaner by having it so accessible.

Possible Strap and Loop Features.
- Open and Close. Most AT packs are 'top-loaders' meaning you access your gear from an opening at the top of the pack. They are closed either by drawstring or roll top. Draw string is faster to open, roll top is a tighter seal.
- Compression. These straps typically wrap horizontally around the sides of your packs. As you eat your food supply during the week, your food supply will shrink. Compressions straps help keep that loose load snug and close to your back.
- Sternum Straps. This horizontal strap connects your left and right shoulder straps together across your chest, in between your nipples and collar bone. Helps secure the pack on your body. Also, if you ever fall, this strap makes sure you don't slide out of your pack. The buckle sometimes comes integrated with an easy access emergency whistle.
- Trekking Pole Loop. A loop used to hang your trekking poles when not using them.

- Bedroll. Two vertical straps usually on the bottom of the pack. Ideal for securely buckling up a foam sleeping pad.
- Extra. Dangle any extra pieces of gear on small loops with a carabiner. I used extra loops for my camp towel, my spork, maybe some dirty socks, etc. Only need a few.

Suggested Packs.
Here are what are most common to find on the AT. The packs with an asterisk are the packs I would personally shop for on my next thru-hike. Aim to keep your pack around 2 lbs.

- Osprey Packs. The commercial leader of quality backpacking packs. They are the biggest backpacking brand on this list and make up the largest portion of AT packs. They have a great warranty policy, a reasonable price tag, and prioritize comfort and support. Their hip belts and shoulder straps usually have thick and cushy padding. This extra comfort puts them in a slightly heavier category though. I hiked with an Exos 58 for the whole AT and, overall, liked it. The signature concave metal frame was not my favorite though. While it did provide some extra airflow, it felt like a turtle shell protruding far out away from my back. I would probably vote for a little lighter, more minimal pack next time.
- *Granite Gear. Minimal, quality backpacks. No extra pockets or frills. A single roll-top main compartment complete with big mesh exterior pouches and two convenient shoulder pouches. Their straps are thin to cut down on any excess. Despite being minimal, these packs are very

comfortable and provide a big bang for your buck. For around $200 retail, they make some of the most affordable, yet quality, thru-hiking packs. Note their new packs have hip belt pockets. Wahoo!

- *Hyperlite Mountain Gear. An ultralight icon. Made out of high-tech Cuben Fiber material, HMG packs are under 2 lbs. and durable workhorses. They have a roll top load and are almost entirely waterproof. Think of these as the king of minimal thru-hiking packs. For around $300 though, you will pay for the luxury.
- *ULA-Equipment. Ultralight, yet less expensive than HMG. Instead of Cuben fiber, ULA uses rip stop nylon. Big mesh front pocket, large hip pockets, roll top or draw string loading and a variety of color schemes. They are known for their water bottle holsters on the front shoulder straps which can be super convenient.
- *Gossamer Gear. Another great ultralight pack manufacturer. Similar compartment, material and pockets as ULA, except the top load is rather unique. It is a foldable flap that allows for easy adjusting depending on your pack volume - complete with a small zipper pouch to store anything that does not fit in the hip pockets. Personal favorite features are the easy stowe holsters for trekking poles and the removable back panel pad. The pad makes for an easy seat on a rough surface.
- Gregory Packs. By far the heaviest pack manufacturer on this list. Their claim to fame is their load carrying capacity and easy access pockets. These are nearly twice as heavy as some

other packs, but can also sustain a load twice as heavy. They have a lot of pockets for organization and well cushioned padding.
- Other Noteworthy Pack Manufacturers: Mountain Laurel Designs, REI, ZPacks.

Pack Cover (or Liner).

Some packs are more water resistant than others. Even the most water resistant packs need an additional barrier to prevent water from accessing your gear.

Pack Cover.
A pack cover is like an external shell or rain cover that wraps around your pack. Some packs come with one included. Otherwise, you can find a generic cover based to match the size of your pack.

The problem with a cover is that they leave the back exposed. Water can run down that tricky spot in between your neck and the back of the pack. Enough rain and your gear can still get wet.

Pack Liner.
I hiked for years with a pack cover until I discovered trash compactor bags and used them like pack liners. A little thicker than regular trash bags, trash compactor bags line the inside of your pack and all gear goes inside them. It's like a giant plastic bag for all gear. I highly recommend getting one. I shipped my pack cover back home as soon as possible and used one trash compactor bag for my entire thru-hike.

Poncho.
We'll cover ponchos more in the rain gear section of the clothing chapter. These can double (or triple) as a pack cover, rain shell and shelter.

Shelter (aka 'Tent').

Freestanding Tents.
By definition, freestanding tents don't require stakes and guylines to stand. Instead of stakes, they come with poles that act as a skeleton-like frame. They rely on the tension created from their flexibility to stand. I went with a one-man freestanding tent (Big Agnes) and overall, enjoyed it.

Pros.
- Flexible location. Can stand up on its own anywhere.
- Sturdy. Able to handle heavier winds and harsher weather.
- Easily Moved. While fully setup, I could pick my freestanding tent up over my head and shake out debris or move it to another spot if need be.
- Easy Setup. The poles generally pop together easily and just need to be clipped onto the tent.

Cons.
- Heavier. Those poles add weight.
- More expensive (maybe). Those poles cost money honey.

Non-Freestanding Tents.
These require guylines and stakes to stand and utilize your trekking poles (instead of poles designed exclusively

for the tent).

Pros.
- Lightweight. Without poles, these puppies can almost get down to a scant pound.

Cons.
- Complicated Setup. The guylines and stakes can take an extra minute to adjust to the right amount of tension.
- Need Trekking Poles. Not a problem for most thru-hikers, but worth considering.
- Inflexible location. Those much needed stakes cannot be driven into a wooden tent platform or hard rocky surfaces and are ineffective on soft soil or sand.

Tent Features to Consider.
- Bathtub Floor. Your tent will have two types of fabrics: tarp like fabric and mesh like fabrics. The tarp will be used to repel water and the mesh will be for ventilation. A bathtub floor means the tarp like fabric lines the floor and at least a few inches above the ground before it meets the mesh walls. This mini tarp like 'bathtub' can be helpful in heavy rains.
- Space. If you are hiking with a partner, get a 2 man tent. Otherwise, most people hike with a 1 man. Some are more spacious than others. Not a huge deal for me though. The tent is really just for sleeping.
- Weight. A lightweight free standing solo tent hovers in the low 2 lb. range, non-freestanding in the low 1 lb. range.

- Single or Double Walled. Double walled tents have a separate rain fly that hovers a few inches above the mesh walls. They are drier than a single wall, but the extra material means more weight.
- Vestibule. Think of these like a mini 'porch' of your tent. They usually only provide a few square feet of cover, but can be nice to keep your bag under instead of cramping it inside the tent. Not recommended, but a vestibule can be handy to cook under on rainy days.
- Pockets. Not necessary. But, one or two internal pockets to stash your headlamp or water bottle at night is ideal.
- Poles. Tents designed with several poles generally maximize more space. I vote less poles though. Less to maintain, less chance of breaking and easier to setup.
- Shape. Some tents are shaped like a teepee pyramid and others more like half-spherical igloos. They come in countless other unique forms. Mostly a matter of personal preference and ease of entry.

Hammocks.

Yes! Roughly one in five AT thru-hikers sleeps in a hammock instead of a tent. Backpacking hammocks are not like your typical cotton webbed, front porch lounger though. Your body hangs in a thin nylon sheet and is covered by a bug proof mesh. Most hammock shelters come with a separate rain tarp as well. When fully setup, it will look like a suspended cocoon or mini tree fort. There is a war between hammocks and tents and you too will swear allegiance someday. Let's break it down.

Pros.
- Dry. All of that bathtub floor talk with tents does
  not apply. In a hammock, you are elevated above
  the wet and soggy ground.
- Lightweight. Some hammock systems are
  extremely light. After all, there are no poles. It is
  just fabric and rope (or straps).
- Comfortable (maybe). The hard ground of a tent is
  much less comfortable than a hammock for some
  hikers.
- Rough Ground. You can setup a hammock above
  rocky, soft, uneven, prickly - any kind of surface.

Cons.
- Cold. Your underside is exposed to the flowing
  air. This can require an extra under quilt in winter
  time to keep you warm.
- Sleeping Position. You are fixed on your back. No
  side or stomach sleeping. Personally, this is the
  main problem I can see with a hammock.
- Less space. Your gear needs to be stored below
  you on the ground or sprawled out inside your
  hammock with you. This is not a comfortable
  space to pack up your gear or change clothes in
  either.
- Trees. Yea, you gotta have trees to tie it up. The
  AT is heavily forested though so this is not a big
  problem. However, there were a few times I
  enjoyed stargazing from my tent on treeless balds.

Hammock Features to Consider.
- Suspension System. The method your hammock

will be hung to the tree. You can use a DIY rope or buy a setup suspension system. Two system options: 1) a whoopie sling which utilizes a loop and knot and is extremely adjustable and 2) straps which contain several fixed loops to easily clip a carabiner to.

- Space. More space means more comfort to roll around in.

My Hammock Experience.
I did not thru-hike with a hammock. For some reason, I never even knew to consider a hammock system before the AT.

If I were to pursue a hammock, I would look into Kammok. While slightly heavier, they are known for some of the most comfortable hammocks on the market. Some models are more spacious and allow asymmetrical sleeping (so you can sprawl out in a variety of positions), while others are ultralight and compact. Complete with a rainfly, bug net and ultralight straps.

ENO, Hennessy Hammocks, Grand Trunk and Warbonnet are some brands to look into as well.

Tarps.

Alright ultralight folks, going to stop you here. Tarps are just that - a tarp. This minimal shelter can be propped up by your trekking poles or strung along between two trees.

Sounds cool. But, no walls and no floor?

I tried sleeping under just my rain fly like a tarp a few times and it was miserable. Spiders crawled across my face several times and mosquitoes feasted on my exposed arms. I may sound like a big fat baby, but I don't like bugs touching me in my sleep. In a hard rain, these things would be even more miserable. Wet ground and possibly some runoff is no fun. Therefore, I just don't find tarps by themselves practical on the AT.

Footprint.

Same thing as a ground cloth. A footprint is used to place directly on the ground below your tent to protect the floor of your tent. It also acts as a moisture barrier on wet ground. Most tent manufacturers make one to match each model of their tents, but it is usually sold separately. They have holes that line up with the tent poles or buckles to clip directly into the rain fly. A tent manufacturer's footprint can cost over $50 though. What?! I know. Let's save some money now (and weight!).

How to Make Your Own Footprint.
I went to the hardware store and bought a 2mm plastic painter's tarp for $2.99. Some people use Tyvek. I sprawled the big 9 x 12 rectangular tarp out on my basement floor and setup my tent on top of it. I got a marker and traced the outline of my tent floor.

You want your footprint to be slightly smaller than the floor of your tent so runoff water does not collect in between the tent floor and the footprint. Therefore, I cut inside my marker line about two inches to make my footprint perimeter smaller than the outline of the tent floor. The result rolled up to the size of a deck of cards, lasted the entire Trail and cost a few bucks.

Trekking Poles.

I suffered a lot before reaching my first outfitter for not packing these. Most of what I read talked about how trekking poles were for beginner hikers and just extra weight. I never used them in Boy Scouts either, so why bring them? A week of agonizing knee pain while hiking followed by several days of ice baths is why.

If there is anything you take away from this book, *please start with trekking poles.* We'll call this the "Save the Knees" campaign. If you don't need your poles after a week or two, fine. Send 'em home and let your strong knees roam free.

Pole Advantages.
- Distribute Weight. Get your body and pack weight off your knees and on your arms some.
- Balance. Poles helped prevent me from falling at slippery river crossings, log bridges, rocks, steep downhills, muddy patches, etc.
- Flow. There is something about having all four limbs working in tandem on the hike. Poles help with that rhythm.
- Protection. One of my most 'vicious' wildlife attacks happened in Maine. I heard a loud rumble in the bushes next to me. It was convinced it was either a silverback gorilla's mating call or a massive black bear hidden three feet away under some flowers. I was terrified and confused. A

small chicken like bird flew out from the brush and head-butted by shin. My trekking pole helped whack it away. It was a very territorial grouse. Grouse make bizarrely deep rumbles on the ground with their feathers (wtf, I know). A trekking pole will help act as a barrier in the rare occasion you accidentally get too close to any grouse, snakes, or any aggressive wildlife really.

- Spider Webs. First on the Trail in the morning? You will take lots of webs to the face. Use the trekking poles.
- Official Jabber. If you see a muddy patch in front and you are not sure how deep it is, jab the poles to see.
- Tent Poles (maybe). Your tent may utilize your trekking poles.

Locking Mechanism.
Unlike, say a golf club, you want poles that collapse. They will come in two or three piece sections. Two piece sections don't collapse as small as three. Two piece poles have less moving parts though and therefore, less probability of breaking.

When extended to your ideal hiking length, there are three main ways manufacturers 'lock' these sections of pole in place: a flip lock, a twist lock or an unfold-and-slide lock. A flip lock is like a small clip that folds over. A twist lock has you twist the individual pole sections in opposing directions. A folding lock is connected by an internal rope and, when extended and aligned, they slide and lock into place (like tent poles). I have never used folding locks and cannot attest. They seem less flexible on length, potentially more fragile, and don't collapse inside themselves though.

Flip locks are easy and probably last longer than the twist lock.

Shock Absorbers.
Gettin' real nerdy now. These soften the weight you place on your poles, and subsequent arms, as you hike. Just like a car, it is a spring-loaded cushion located at the joints of the pole sections. An unnecessary fancy feature that causes more harm than good in my opinion. That extra inch or two movement from the spring makes me feel unstable.

Weight and Material.
Your pair of poles should weigh around 1 lb. or less... or about 6-8 oz. per pole. Get Carbon Fiber or Aluminum. Aluminum is generally a tad stronger and more flexible while carbon fiber is lighter. To me though, the differences are negligible.

Grips.
- Cork. Most popular. Molds to the shape of your hand. Nice 'natural' feel. The middle weight option.
- Foam. Comfortable, lightweight and possibly less friction on your hands. Can get spongy when wet and retain odor. Less durable.
- Rubber. My favorite. Does not absorb water nor any oil from your hands. Has a little more insulation which makes it better for winter. Heaviest option.

Pole Tips.
The end point of your trekking pole that actually makes contact with the ground. Some poles provide mini rubber shoe-like tips with about a square inch surface area. I

prefer tiny metal tips about twice the size of the lead tip of a pencil. The sharp point is helpful to grip small contours of a rock or stab into a slick surface. My tips lasted nearly 2,000 miles before needing to be replaced.

Baskets.
You might be more familiar with the baskets on ski poles. They are plastic circles fixed about 4 inches above the pole tip. They should help prevent your pole from jabbing too deep into soft ground. The wider the basket, the more they prevent you from sliding into the ground. Big baskets are obviously a bit clunkier and heavier and may gather more leaves from the ground. Really just personal preference.

Of all my gear, I spent the least amount of time researching my trekking poles. Basically because I knew anything would be better than the fat logs I had been using... and there were only a few options at the store. I ended up purchasing a pair of $35 Tubbs ski poles which were not even designed for hiking. 2 sections with a twist lock, big baskets and rubber handles. Twist lock was not the best and, at times, was nearly impossible to collapse. This meant dealing with fully extended poles most of the time. Otherwise, the same pair worked well for the whole Trail.

Sleeping Bag and Liner.

Down or Synthetic Insulation?
One of the biggest backpacking debates. Down feathers are lighter, warmer and pack smaller than synthetic insulation options. Down has an Achilles heel though - it loses loft and insulation ability when wet. Losing

insulation is a scary thought for winter backpacking. Down is also expensive. 'Fill-power' is a measurement of the warmth to weight ratio. Typically ranges from 600 to 950. The higher the number, the more 'quality' the feather insulation.

I kept my sleeping bag well protected in a waterproof stuff sack and a waterproof pack liner and never had a water issue. A few roof leaks in shelters might have dripped on my bag, but nothing to significantly affect the insulation ability. If you can afford it and will keep it protected, I vote go for down insulation.

Warmth.
Try to think of the degree ratings as only accurate for survival situations. Example: if you see "(Ultimate Bag) 20", that means you will be able to survive in the sleeping bag if the temperature drops to 20 degrees Fahrenheit. This is a much lower threshold than what is actually *comfortable* to sleep in though. For me, I'd add at least 20 degrees to the manufacturer's claim for a comfortable night sleep. Therefore, for that same 20 degree bag example, I'd probably only feel comfortable sleeping in it in 40 degree weather without an additional liner or clothes.

I used a synthetic 15 degree bag and would have liked even warmer in winter. I needed two liners and still slept very cold on late November and early December nights. Cold nights suck. If you are committed to hiking in the warmest months, a 30 or 35 degree bag is probably best. Otherwise, if you are starting NOBO in early February or ending SOBO in late November, I recommend a 0 or 15 degree bag.

Weight.
Depending on how warm your bag is and how much you are willing to spend, your sleeping bag should be between 1 and 3 lbs.

Do I need 2 sleeping bags for summer and winter?
Meh, not really. Sounds expensive. If in doubt, I vote err on the warm side and get a full-on winter bag. A winter bag can be compatible in summer, but a summer bag just won't cut it in winter. If the thick winter sleeping bag is too hot on summer nights, unzip it or just sleep in your bag liner.

Mummy or Quilt?
Mummy bags are the traditional cocoon like sleeping bags with an added head wraps that only leave your smiling face exposed. These are warm, but can be constricting and don't allow a wide range of sleeping positions. Their zippers can be a pain to get in and out of as well.

Quilts are like big insulated blankets. Some are completely rectangular and have no zippers at all. Others are sort of a half breed with a foot box to tuck your feet into and some straps or clips to close the open wall of the blanket. Quilts generally allow more movement, but may not provide as much of a snug enclosure as desired.

Sleeping Bag Liner.
I love 'em. They add insulation to your sleeping bag on colder nights… or serve as a thin blanket on hot nights. Think of them as sheet-like sleeping bags that you slip into before getting into your actual sleeping bag. Usually cotton, silk or fleece, they can be much more comfortable on contact with your skin than the synthetic walls of your

sleeping bag. The liner also blocks your sweaty and grimy skin from dirtying up your less-than-easy-to-clean sleeping bag.

I hiked with a Sea to Summit sleeping bag liner that came coated in Insect Shield. It was polyester, but felt as cozy as cotton. Good stuff.

Sleeping Pads.

There are two main options: foam sleeping pads and inflatable sleeping pads.

Foam Pads.
These either roll up or fold up. They are exactly what they sound like - a rectangular piece of soft foam similar to a yoga mat. Their grooves can range for comfort, compactness and style.

Pros.
- Easy. Just throw it down and spread your sleeping bag on top.
- Indestructible. I used to love relaxing on my foam pad by the fire not worrying if an ember might fly out and pop my pad. Same thing for rocky or jagged surfaces.
- Cheap. Usually less, if not a lot less, than $50.

Cons
- Bulky. They might take up half of the inside of your bag. Therefore, most hikers have them tied down on top of their pack or flopping around underneath.

- Uncomfortable (maybe). Some people just can't sleep on them. Others prefer the stiff sleep.

Inflatable Pads.
Either self-inflation or manual inflation. The differences are rather insignificant and can vary from model to model. Self-inflating pads fill up with air on their own. Just unroll them on the ground, open the valve and watch them slowly rise. Otherwise, you will manually inflate the pad with good 'ole lung power. There are lightweight pumps out there. I never saw anyone using a pump though and I would think they are unnecessary.

Pros.
- Compact. My pad conveniently rolled up to almost the size of a water bottle.
- Comfortable. The air in inflatable pads elevates you off the ground and provides a nice cushion. For side and stomach sleeper, this is crucial.

Cons.
- Punctures. Even inflatable pads can take a decent beating. Mine has lasted several years without a puncture. You will still need to be careful about where you place your pad though. They can pop any moment from a sharp edge, a fire ember or just heavy wear.
- Inflation. Some pads need a lot of breaths to completely fill up.
- Noisy (maybe). Some inflatable pads are 'crinkly' right out of the package. I knew a lot of hikers that shipped their pads back to the manufacturer because they were too noisy. My pad was a noisy one. However, just like most new gear, it only

needed a lil' tender loving to break it in. After a few nights, the noise was gone entirely.

Both Similar.

- Insulation. Be sure to check the "R-Value" which is a scale used to measure how well the pad insulates your body heat. Aim to keep your pad above 3 for winter time. A high R-value will act as a barrier and prevent the cold ground from reaching you and sucking away precious body heat. Other than comfort, insulation is the main reason I use a sleeping pad.
- Weight. Your pad should not weigh more than 1 lb. Foam pads have been traditionally viewed as a lighter option than inflatable. That is not always the case though. They can vary by model and manufacturer. At 12 oz., my inflatable pad was lighter than most foam pads.

I grew up backpacking with foam pads as a kid. However, I decided to get an inflatable pad for my thru-hike (Therm-a-Rest NeoAir). The foam pads were just too uncomfortable and obnoxiously bulky to carry around. My NeoAir was tiny, ultralight and pretty comfortable. My only complaint was inflating it every night. After hours of hiking, pushing my lungs into a pad would literally make me dizzy. Note I never carried a repair kit and never need one.

Sea to Summit makes some ultralight and warm rivals to the NeoAir. They weigh a hair more than the NeoAir, but make up for it in comfort. I have never slept on a pad more comfortable than a Sea to Summit mat.

Pillow.

No puffy pillows, not even travel size. Some hikers wad up their unworn clothes into a lump, some use a thin fleece liner to mold their clothes into a pillow shape, and some don't even use a pillow.

I preferred a little more comfort and chose a Therm-a-Rest stuff sack with a fleece liner. It had a waterproof shell that was great protection while hiking and also inverted to a fleece lined sack while sleeping. The fleece felt great on my cheek at night and the stuff sack shell provided a firmer container for the clothes. I could also 'fluff' the clothes to give them some more loft if they ever flattened down too much. The sack was entirely washable.

Another pillow option is to go inflatable. You may appreciate the loft and enjoy a better night sleep. These can add 2-6 oz. to your pack though. There are a lot of options depending on how you sleep.

Despite enjoying the Therm-a-rest, I would go for a Sea to Summit inflatable pillow next thru-hike. At 2.5 oz, they weigh almost nothing and are the most comfortable backpacking pillow I have ever felt. It's like resting your head on a cloud. A better night sleep is always worth it to me. Check out Cocoon, NEMO, REI, Exped or Klymit options as well.

Stove and Fuel.

Ahhh, your heavenly stove. Bringing heat to your sometimes monotonous meal plan. Please bring one. A stove is only as good as its fuel source though.

(Most Common) Canister Fuel/ Screw Top Stove.
In my opinion, by far the best way to go. I used a Snow
Peak GigaPower. Jetboils are a little different, but popular
as well.

The stove top is pronged and folds up small enough to fit
in your pocket. The fuel source is a pressurized canister
that screws on underneath.

- Stable surface to cook on.
- Adjustable flame for a simmer or full on boil.
- No lighter needed (maybe). Many have a built in
  lighter spark that is as easy as clicking a button
  (called a 'Piezo Ignition').
- Canister fuel is readily available along the AT.
- Strong flame to fight against heavy wind.
- Slightly heavier than some other stove options.

Note an easy way to see how much fuel is left in the
canister is to let it float in water. The part sticking above
water will be the 'air' in the canister and indicate how
much has been consumed.

(Common) Alcohol Fuel/ Tin Can Stove.
Some companies make these stoves. They are more often
made from a Do-It-Yourself beer or soda can with holes
punched in the sides though. Pour alcohol into the can
chamber and then ignite the fuel.

- Ultralight. Weighs almost nothing.
- Cheap and accessible fuel.
- Messy. Alcohol can get all over stuff. When

finished cooking, your can is often left with alcohol to wipe out.
- Unstable (and potentially dangerous). Typically very flimsy and unstable making them dangerous if they get knocked over when lit.
- Weak and inflexible flame. These have one setting - low. Not ideal for windy conditions.

(Less Common) Liquid Fuel/ Pump and Stand Stove.
A bottle containing fuel (white gas or kerosene) connects to the stove top from a chord. You manually create pressure inside the bottle with a mini pump.

- Stable surface to cook on.
- Cheap and flexible fuel. White gas, kerosene, unleaded gasoline.
- Large flame. Great for hiking partners and group cooking.
- Best option for below freezing conditions.
- Refillable bottle.
- Require a lot of maintenance, pumping, and complicated parts.
- Heaviest stove option.

(Rare) Wood or Tab Fuel/ Stand Stove.
A collapsible stove frame acts like a mini fire pit. You place twigs inside the frame and make a small fire. I only want to mention these as an option because some people do actually use them.

They are very impractical for a thru-hike in my opinion though. Wet wood is a constant issue and maintaining a steady flame with a miniature fire is a delicate art. I'd rather just set my pot directly in the fire pit than fiddle with a baby fire inside a tiny metal box.

Windscreen.
I thought a windscreen would add unnecessary weight.
On the contrary, I came to learn how important they are to
increase fuel efficiency… especially in winter. Your
canister fuel flows much slower in cold weather. Not to
mention that your stove is already fighting an uphill battle
against heating colder water and a colder pot. The
combination can drain your fuel while your water
slooowly heats up.

A double folded piece of aluminum foil will act as a
windscreen - effectively blocking the wind and channeling
the flame to heat your pot much more efficiently.

Fuel Duration.
Adjustable fuel sources (alcohol, liquid, etc.) will vary
depending on how much you chose to pack out. Canisters
have a fixed amount of fuel. They generally come in 4, 8
and 16 oz. single-use containers. 16 oz. is too heavy to
pack. The 4 and 8 oz. are a reasonably volume to carry. I
found that a 4 oz. canister would last about a week. At that
weekly rate, I was using just enough to bring 500 ml of
water to a boil once a day.

Cooking Pot (or Cup).

Notice "pot" is singular. Don't pack a kitchen set with
several plates, cups and pots. You only need one pot or
cup with a lid. The majority of your cooking will probably
be just boiling water.

Size and Weight.
I recommend getting a cup able to hold at least 1 liter of water. That will give you enough volume for a full dehydrated meal, a rice dish or a large cup of tea. Your cup or pot should weigh between 4-8 oz.

Materials.
I don't think it makes much difference honestly. All of these metals have lightweight pot and cup options that will boil your water just fine. Some small differences:
- Titanium. The lightest of them all and stronger than aluminum. Titanium is known for heating quickly and, subsequently, getting too hot and burning things.
- Stainless Steel. The strongest and heaviest option. Able to take a beating with minimal, or no, scratching.
- Aluminum. The best for actual cooking. It distributes heat most evenly. The least durable option though and can require a little more non-stick maintenance.
- Cast Iron. Way too heavy. Don't bring it.

Grip and Handles.
Get a pot or cup with a handle. Something that folds away nicely, but stable enough to carry when full of food or water. Some pots and cups have rubber covered handles and lids and mouth pieces to prevent your fingers or lips from getting burned. I vote ditch the rubber. The rubber covers only prevent you from being able to set it in the fire. Use your towel or bandana to maneuver the pot or wait a minute for it to cool down if need be.

Consider a Kettle.

I had never thought of these until my hiking partner busted one out. She used to boil water with a tea kettle placed directly in the heart of the fire. It was so convenient to just drop the kettle, walk away and come back to boiling water. Since we made a fire every night (and some mornings) in winter, this saved a lot of fuel. The kettle was also a lot more stable than my cup which would often get knocked over when I placed it in the fire.

The drawback is that the kettle is an extra item - i.e. you need an additional cup to drink from or eat your food in. Also, I rarely made fires in summer making them only helpful in winter.

Utensil.

Same as the pot, you don't need a complicated kitchen set of forks, knives and spoons. One spork will do. Get titanium for the reason that it is light and strong. The 'hot spot' problem of titanium is much less relevant with your spork.

I highly recommend getting a full size utensil. There are plenty of 'keychain sporks' out there that ain't gonna cut it. You want a handle able to extend deep into the food packaging to prevent dirtying up your fingers. Even a full size utensil should only weigh a fraction of an ounce.

Some hikers carried a multi-use plastic utensil with a spoon on one end and a serrated fork on the other. These have a larger spoon scoop than most metallic sporks. I feel like the serrated end on the fork is pointless though. It is not enough to really cut through anything and is rough on your mouth. If you need to cut something, you will use your pocket knife anyway.

I liked my Sea to Summit spork. It came with a small hole and a carabiner hooked through it. It stayed clipped on the outside of my pack for easy access. The ruler straight handle was helpful for scraping any mess out of my pot as well.

Knife.

Do I need a knife?
Yes. You will want to cut up food, open packaging, repair gear and do lots of other random things. Carrying a knife gave me a small sense of protection in the extremely rare case I was in fact attacked by something - man or animal. It was also comforting to have in the extremely rare case of a survival situation.

Don't go Rambo.
Unless you want to grease up your biceps and take some selfies, you don't need a foot long stainless-steel survival knife with a leather sheath. No 20 function multi-tool either. Just a single collapsible blade. Maybe a 3 inch stainless-steel blade. Keep it around 2-3 oz.

No Razorblades.
The ultralight crowd might vote for a razor blade instead of a knife. I find these way too impractical to do virtually anything with though.

I hiked with a Gerber EVO and was happy with it. It was

easy to open, had a durable handle, a quality blade, unlocked and folded easily, and weighed less than 3 oz.

Towel.

Helpful for wiping off your hands, wiping out a dirty dish, picking a hot pot off the stove, drying your feet at a river crossing or drying your entire body at a pond. Get a camp towel instead of a cotton rag or bandana. They are much more absorbent and most have some anti-microbial treatment to cut down on the stink.

I used a small PackTowl that unfolded to about one square foot. It came with a loop to button on the side of my pack and dry out as I hiked.

Stuff Sacks.

Why are stuff sacks important?
Instead of a clunky commercial pack with unnecessary pockets and compartments, most thru-hikers prefer minimal backpacks paired with some stuff sacks. You can get a stuff sack tiny enough just to protect your cell phone as well as get one big enough to line your entire pack.

- Compartmentalize. Proper organization saves a lot of headache. Reaching for your stove as hunger strikes, grabbing an extra layer when the sun sets, etc.
- Waterproof. It is always good to add an extra layer of protection to your gear. Even after a heavy rain, stuff sacks ensure your clothes, sleeping bag and electronics are dry when you reach camp.

- Portability. It is much easier to bring your stuff sack to the campfire than your entire pack.

I used four stuff sacks - all different colors, sizes and closures.

1. Food Stuff Sack.

I used a Sea to Summit stuff sack for my food. It has 15 liters of carrying capacity and a drawstring closure. The drawstring made it easy to open and great for hanging on mouse lines and bear bagging. The sack uses Cordura fabric which is durable and very water resistant. It comfortably fits about a week's worth of food and weighs about 1 ounce.

2. Gear Stuff Sack.

I stored all my 'mini gear' in an Outdoor Research stuff sack. It carried things like my headlamp, stove and cup, journal, eBook, toiletries and first aid kit. It has 10 liters of carrying capacity and a roll top closure. The roll top is great for an almost submersible waterproof seal. It has a small plastic loop to hook on to nails in the shelters. It weighs about 2 oz. I recommend shaving an ounce and going for a lighter drawstring sack similar to the food sack above.

3. Clothes Stuff Sack.

Unless I was hanging a wet and stinky pair of socks off the back of my pack, anything I was not wearing was stuffed in my clothes sack. It usually stayed at the bottom of my pack until reaching camp. Drawstring closure and 10-15 liters capacity. As mentioned, my clothes stuff sack also doubled as my pillow.

4. Sleeping Bag Stuff Sack.

More than any other stuff sack, this one needs to have a compression option. Your sleeping bag will be too big and puffy to float around your pack. You can store it in a stuff sack with a roll top or one with compression straps or both. Generally roll tops are good for the tight enclosure (waterproof, bug proof) and compressing small.

My Mountain Hardwear bag came with a good stuff sack with 3 lightweight vertical compression straps. Stuff the sleeping bag in the sack, close the sack (roll top or drawstring) and then tighten each strap little by little until the sleeping bag is as dense as it can get.

No Tent Stuff Sacks.

My Big Agnes tent came with a stuff sack for the tent, one for the stakes, and one for the poles. The tent compressed easily enough to mash in the bottom of my pack and the poles folded up nicely on the side of my pack. Therefore, I just did not need either of those stuff sacks. I did, however, use their stakes sack for stakes and my footprint.

Bring Plastic Bags.

I used a handful of ziploc bags to compartmentalize gear within the stuff sacks. Separating things like my first aid kit from my toiletries was super helpful. I also always carried a spare bag or two to reseal a brick of cheese, etc.

Headlamp.

No flashlights please. You need that light beam to be hands free to use while hiking, cooking or digging around your tent at night.

Lumens and Beam Distance.
Lumens is a unit to measure the *amount* of light the
headlamp puts out. One lumen is a standard measurement
of the light a candle emits during a single second. The
higher the lumens, the more light your headlamp emits.
Note this can be in any direction. As you can imagine, a 70
lumen light bulb will emit light very differently than 70
lumen spotlight.

This is where beam distance matters. Beam distance
measures how *far* the light goes. The combination of
lumens and beam distance will give you an idea of how
powerful your headlamp is. Keep in mind the more
powerful headlamps usually drain batteries at a faster
rate.

Some ultralight hikers are fine with a small 20 lumen
lamp. I prefer a little more power… like 50-100 lumens
and a beam distance of 50-100 meters. A handful of times I
hiked at night with fog so thick I could barely see my feet.
Even on clear nights, there is a level of comfort that comes
with a strong beam. Being able to see down a hill, through
the trees or scope out a river crossing are some situations
where I really appreciated that strong beam.

Beam Settings.
- Flood and Spot. Headlamps come with either a
  spotlight or flood setting. Most headlamps now
  provide both options to toggle between. The flood
  setting provides low intensity and broad light -
  like the lightbulb from a lamp. The spot setting
  provides a high intensity and sharp beam of light -
  like the spotlight from an on stage theater
  performance.

- Signal Beacon. This is a flicker setting to be used as an emergency beacon. Thankfully, I never used this. It is comforting to have though.
- Red Option. I used the red light option more than any other setting. The dim red light might feel a bit strange - like you are in a military operation. But, it is very low-intensity and therefore, drains a minimal amount of battery. The red option is great for close range activities at camp like reading and journaling where your other setting could be blinding... or just drain too quickly.

Physical Properties.
- Strap. Some use an ultralight retractable string. My headlamp might have been on the heavier end. But, it had a comfortable elastic band about two inches wide that helped keep it secured on my head without cutting off any circulation.
- Weight. Should be about 3 oz.
- Battery Life. Manufacturers can be misleading on the battery hours listed. Let's say the 100 lumen headlamp is listed at 60 hours of battery life at maximum output. That leads me to believe that I will have 100 lumens for 60 hours. Ehh, not really. That means at the maximum setting, it will start out emitting 60 lumens of light and slowly die down to nothing after 100 hours. My headlamp used three AAA batteries which needed to be replaced a couple times a month. If you can find a rechargeable headlamp that is compatible with a charger you are already bringing, I recommend going rechargeable. The battery will be less powerful. But, maintaining a supply of spares is worse.

- Water Resistant. There is a standard rating system used to measure the level of water resistance of electronics. You will see "IP X" followed by a number from 0 to 8 in the product description. As a point of reference: 0 means no resistance at all to water, 4 means it can handle splashing water and 8 means it is completely submersible. Go for one between 4 and 8.
- Tilt. Having a headlamp that can adjust to different angles is fairly standard. Be sure your headlamp can tilt in a few positions and is not fixed in place.

I hiked with a Black Diamond and it lasted my entire hike. Petzl makes great headlamps. I would go with Princeton Tec next time though for their lower profile, horizontal design and easily adjustable angle positions.

Toiletries.

Toothbrush.
I think I started off with a toothbrush with a sawed off handle. It was impractical. I ended up with a 2 piece travel toothbrush from Wal Mart. Knowing how dirty things can get in my pack, I liked having the bottom cap piece to store and protect the top brush piece.

Toothpaste.
A 1 ounce travel tube will work. Instead of always buying new little travel tubes, I would re-use them. I would bounce forward a big tube of toothpaste and use it to refill my travel tube. Match up the circular tips and squeeze toothpaste from the big tube into the little tube.

Toilet Paper.

Don't leave home without it. I would often take a few feet from the hostel, hotel or a restaurant in town. You can bounce box a favorite roll to the next town as well.

Soap.

Hand sanitizer only. As mentioned, do any dishes and personal bathing in town. The hand sanitizer will ensure you have clean hands before eating and after using the bathroom. It also doubled as deodorant and foot wipe when particularly dirty.

Bugspray.

Bugs and creepy crawlies are a somewhat inevitable sanity test. The mosquitoes and blackflies can be overwhelming at times. Bug spray seems futile to some. I disagree though. It will, at minimum, lessen the severity of the black fly and mosquito attacks. Spraying some around your socks will help prevent ticks (and Lyme Disease) as well. I have found DEET and Picaridin to be the most effective repellents. Get as close to 100% concentration for DEET and 20% concentration for Picaridin as possible.

I also coated all of my clothes, tent and sleeping bag in Permethrin before leaving. This coating can repel bugs up to 6 weeks on some fabrics. See Sawyer products.

First Aid Kit.

You are not preparing for Armageddon or a deep-tissue operation. You are, however, preparing for common injuries and illnesses.

- Small plastic bag. Maybe 4x6 inches. I liked

keeping my first aid items separate from everything else. They are small and can get lost easily otherwise.

- 2 ft. of Duct Tape. Get an old pen, take the ink stick cartridge out, and cut the hollow shaft of the pen in half. Wrap duct tape around the pen. When finished, it will be about the size of a AA battery. Beyond the obvious gear uses of duct tape, it can be used for a variety of first aid applications - like taping up blister hot spots or securing band aids.
- Pain Relievers. Carry about 6-10 pills. There are two types of OTC (over the counter) pain relievers to choose from: 1) acetaminophen (Tylenol) and 2) non-steroidal anti-inflammatory (Ibuprofen and Aspirin). Both have pros and cons. I had several aches and pains as well as swollen knees and ankles at times. Therefore, I prefer Ibuprofen or Aspirin for the pain relief AND anti-inflammatory.
- Anti-Diarrhea. Maybe 6 pills. Medications like Imodium.
- Lip Balm. Use the Vaseline from your fire kit or carry lip balm separately. I used lip balm to grease up and reduce friction on the hot spots of my feet, heels, in between toes, etc. Use your finger instead of rubbing chapstick directly on your feet ;)
- Baby Powder. On the contrary, baby powder is to dry out steamy 'under the garment' spots. I did not chaff a lot on the AT, but baby powder saved the day when I did.
- Antiseptic Wipe. Used to clean small wounds before dressing them with a bandaid.
- Band Aids. I needed a lot of these. At least 4 new ones everyday around my toes to minimize

blisters. Toe socks might help prevent the blisters.

Fire Kit.

Fires repel bugs and dry out wet socks in summer. Their heat is magnetic in winter. Most of the time a lighter and some dry grass was all I needed to start a fire. However, if it had been raining, having this fire kit was the only hope I had to get something started.

A small container of Vaseline, a dozen cotton balls and a mini Bic lighter. Swipe a cotton ball into a glob of Vaseline and stick it in the heart of your firewood frame and then light. The cotton balls are dry and quick to catch. The petroleum jelly (Vaseline) is slow-burning enough to help ignite the thicker sticks in the pile. Man makes fire.

Map.

We talked about AWOL and The Thru-Hiker's Companion. To save weight, I ripped out a couple hundred miles worth of pages at a time and bounced forward the remaining sections of the book. I kept these few pages folded over in a ziploc bag in my pocket as I hiked so I could constantly check how far the next water source, shelter, whatever was.

Little Stuff I Used.

Watch.
A waterproof one from Wal mart with a light button for nighttime. While I did not like constantly knowing what time it was, I did like becoming familiar with my pace. I

began to know almost exactly how far I had hiked based on how long I had been hiking. A watch also provided an occasional early morning alarm.

Earplugs.
One of my most treasured items. I sleep light and these things help drown out loud snorers in the shelters, the mysterious noises in the woods, or possibly even a nearby road.

Wallet.
Or lack thereof. I kept my cash, debit card and ID together with a binder clip.

Paracord.
20-30 ft. Nice to string up as a dry line, repair gear, bear bag, or hang stuff off your pack.

Journal and Pen.
Yes! Bring one. I used a Rite in the Rain journal. They make small and lightweight journals that are extremely weather resistant. Their claim to fame is that you can literally write in them while raining.

Repair Kit.
Just a needle and floss. After a thousand miles, things started to tear. Pockets on my pants, the mesh pouches on my pack, my sleeping bag liner, etc.

My Full Gear List.

This is just what I hiked with. I do NOT recommend all of these and, as noted before, would definitely do a few things differently. I want you to use this though as a point of reference AND to know that you don't need a perfect gear list to complete your thru-hike.

1. Backpack. Osprey Exos 58.
2. Pack Liner. Trash Compactor Bag.
3. Tent. Big Agnes Fly Creek UL 1.
4. Sleeping Bag. Mountain Hardwear Ultralamina 15.
5. Sleeping Bag Liner. Sea to Summit.
6. Sleeping Pad. Term-a-Rest Neo Air Xlite.
7. Stove. Snow Peak Gigapower and Canister Fuel.
8. Stuff Sacks. Outdoor Research 10L, Sea to Summit 15L.
9. Pillow. Therm-a-Rest fleece lined stuff sack.
10. eBook. Amazon Kindle.
11. Phone. A cheap flip one.
12. Headlamp. Black Diamond Spot with AAA batteries.
13. Water Filter. Sawyer Squeeze.
14. Water Containers. Platypus 1L and Smart Water 1L.
15. iPod. Music and audiobooks.
16. Camera. Nikon weatherproof digital camera.
17. Knife. Gerber EVO.
18. Journal. Rite in the Rain.
19. Guide Book. AWOL.
20. Repair Kit. Needle and floss.
21. First Aid Kit. Baby Powder, Pain Medication, Bandaids, Duct Tape, Anti Diarrhea Meds.
22. Toiletries. Toothbrush, toothpaste, toilet paper, hand sanitizer.
23. Fire Kit. Cotton balls, Vaseline, Bic lighter.
24. Bugspray. 2 Oz 100% DEET.

25. Towel. Small Packtowl.
26. Ear Plugs. One pair.
27. Watch. Walmart, water resistant thing-a-ma-jig.
28. Trekking Poles. Tubbs ski poles.
29. Pot. Bought in New Zealand and no idea what brand it is.
30. Utensil. Sea to Summit spork.
31. Hiking Shirts. 2 Starter synthetics from Wal Mart.
32. Shirt Base Layer. Patagonia Long Sleeve Capilene.
33. Boxers. ExoFiccio Briefs.
34. Pants. The North Face zip off pants or Nike Running Shorts.
35. Socks and Liners. Rotated brands. Darn Tough, Fits, Wigwam, REI and Smartwool.
36. Rain Shell. Arcteryx Alpha SL.
37. Mid Layer Jacket. Arcteryx Atom.
38. Camp Shoes. Crocs.
39. Hiking Shoes. Brooks Cascadia or Salewa Firetail.
40. Gaiters. Dirty Girl.
41. Beanie. Arcteryx wool.
42. Headwear. Buff.
43. (winter) Gloves. Got a shell from Cabela's and some thin liners from Wal Mart.
44. (winter) Mid Layer Shirt. Minus 33 wool long sleeve.
45. (winter) Extra base Layer Shirt. Starter synthetic long sleeve from Wal Mart.

CHAPTER 10

Clothing

Overview and Considerations.

Weather.
The weather will be the biggest factor impacting what clothes you decide to bring. As a SOBO, I hiked in blistering 100-degree August days and slept in snowy 0-degree December nights. NOBO's can experience similar extremes as well. This dramatic range in temperature forces to you hike with different sets of clothes for each season. Actually, it was more like the clothes in my pack evolved item by item as the weather transitioned. Don't stress too much about planning what you'll be wearing by the time you finish. You can add or remove clothing items along the way and as you learn more about your personal preferences.

Layering.
For flexibility, most hikers layer their clothes. Instead of going directly from a steamy puffy jacket to a nippy tshirt, layers provide several options in between. The most common example for me was starting the hike on chilly

mornings. I'd typically wear two base layers (long sleeve shirt and tshirt) and a rain shell. As I started exerting more energy and the day warmed up, I would slowly get warmer and warmer. I would peel off the top two layers as needed until I was down to my tshirt in the warmest part of the day. Then add them back on one by one as it cooled down and the sun set in the evening.

Ensuring each layer performs its intended function adequately can be crucial to a comfortable (and safe) hike.

- Base Layer. The clothing closest to, and touching, your skin designed to trap your body heat (shirt).
- Mid Layer. The second layer designed to insulate your body (jacket/ fleece).
- Outer Layer. The exposed layer shielding you from rain and wind (rain jacket/ shell).

Materials.

- Wool Material. It is warm and insulates when wet. It is also fairly odor resistant which can be a big advantage in the shower-less backcountry. A lot of backpacking clothing is 'Merino' which is a specific type of lamb that produces a finer micron follicle. This finer follicle is considered to produce a more quality clothing material versus regular lambswool.
- Synthetic Material. Moisture wicking and fast-drying. Nylon, polyester and polypropylene synthetics are generally more durable and rip resistant than wool. Whether it is raining or you are generating buckets of sweat, the Trail is wet. Therefore, you want to bring some fast-drying synthetic pieces of clothing.
- Cotton Sucks. I know it is comfortable. But, please

don't bring any on your hike. When wet, it does not wick moisture or insulate well.

Break it Up.
Keep in mind what time of day you will be wearing the clothing. I had two completely independent sets of clothes and had zero overlapping items. I HIGHLY recommend you separate your hiking outfit and your sleeping outfit.

- Hiking Outfit. My hiking clothes were generally short sleeved synthetics that would get sweaty and need to dry fast.
- Sleeping Outfit. My camp clothes were long sleeve wool designed to keep me warm as the sun went down and as I rested. These stayed dry at all cost. Having a dry set off clothes to put on at night help maintain my sanity.

Replacement and Durability.
You definitely don't *need* name brands and, in many cases, can get by with items that cost a fraction as much. However, you will wear these clothes almost every day for months on some tough terrain. Name brands will do two things: 1) Provide peace of mind that you didn't buy a piece of junk and 2) probably have a good warranty policy and will replace your gear free of charge. Your shoes will be the most prone to wear and tear and will definitely need to be replaced before you finish. There are plenty of gear stores along the way to shop though as well as mail drops to order new replacements.

Fit.
I like my hiking clothes more snug than my 'real world' clothes. Nothing constricting, just a little less baggy. Why? A few reasons...

- Loose clothes are more prone to snag on branches and thorns.
- A snug fit prevents my clothes from getting twisted and wrapped around crease areas as I hike and take my pack on and off several times throughout the day.
- Baggy clothes have more material and can add a few more ounces to the pack weight.

Summer Clothes.

Headwear.
A bandanna or headband. I hiked with a Buff on my head nearly every day on the AT. It was light and somewhat elastic making it a comfortable and versatile headband. It kept my greasy hair back, prevented sweat from streaming down my face and blocked all sorts of bugs and debris from falling in my hair. The Buff also doubled as a face mask on mornings I wanted to sleep in.

Two Tshirts.
I spent a lot of time researching the best hiking tshirts before my hike and coughed up some good cash for 'the best'. Ultimately, they were just synthetic tshirts with a pretty logo. I switched to some Walmart shirts after a few hundred miles that cost under $10. I would generally wear each shirt for 2 or 3 days of hiking until reaching the next trail town.

Long Sleeve Shirt.
My clean and dry long sleeve shirt (Patagonia capilene) would only be worn at camp once I finished hiking and sweating for the day.

Mid Layer Jacket.
I recommend carrying an insulating mid-layer even in the summer months. You never know what the weather is going to do. If it is a hot night, then use it for a cushy pillow. Since down feathers do not insulate when wet, and your jacket will get wet on the AT, consider a synthetic insulated jacket. They can also be washed much easier than down insulation. I was happy with my Arc'teryx Atom for warmer months. It was comfortable, light and felt great. Please get something warmer, ideally with warmer down insulation, for colder months.

Rain Shell.
There are basically three ways to fight the inevitable rain. You want a hood with a drawstring, or some method of securing it snugly around your face. My hardshell had a miniature bill on it that was nice addition to prevent water from streaming down my face all day.

- Hardshell Jacket. Very durable and can take a beating. They typically have a few materials stacked on top of each other designed to block the rain while, simultaneously, allowing your body to breath and ventilate. Hardshells are thicker and can be very expensive. I used a hardshell (Arc'teryx Alpha SL). However, I was not convinced by its breathability… nor the waterproof abilities. The waterproof coating wore off after a few washes and my body would frequently be wet in heavy rains. Even with arm pit zippers, it did not seem to breathe well at all and I was always super steamy in it. So what's the point in wearing one at all if you are still going to get wet? Well… it was extremely sturdy which was helpful shedding off snow and plowing through the occasionally thick brush. Because it was so durable, I often threw it down on the ground like an iron blanket to lay on, stargaze, whatever.

- Poncho. Like a tarp with a hood for your head. Despite being floppy and all over the place, I would probably use a poncho on my next thru-hike. The biggest advantage of a poncho is that it can cover *everything*. It covers your entire pack and, in particular, that tricky spot in between the back of your neck and your pack which can be a great place for rain to run down. Also, depending on its length, it can channel rain away from your pants. A poncho breaths relatively well because the wide open bottom can circulate air flow.
- Light Rain Jacket. Just what you think. These are lighter than hardshells and much much less expensive. There are many hybrid options which can be more durable than a cheap nylon jacket as well. Be sure to get one with a hood. Rain jackets are typically not breathable at all though and may tear more easily than a hardshell.

Pair of Shorts or Pants.

- Running shorts. Super light, fast drying and breathable. The inner mesh 'pouch' acts as built in underwear as well. They will not keep you warm on chilly mornings or rainy days. They also won't protect your legs from brush. I hiked in running shorts only for a couple months in the dead heat of summer when I was confident the early mornings were still warm.
- Pants. Durable, warm and pocket storage. For anything other than the dead heat of summer, I

hiked with zip off North Face pants. They were synthetic and dried relatively fast. The zip off option gave flexibility to hike cool on warm days or warm on cool days.

2 Pairs of Underwear.
Some people go without it entirely. "You're going to be dirty anyway and underwear just adds weight." Eh, I'm not fully convinced. I hiked with boxer briefs (Exofficio) and found them helpful for two reasons:

Reason 1: Chaffing. Your pants are not designed to make direct contact with your sensitive parts and can cause friction. Underwear also helps separate parts of your skin from other parts of your skin and, again, reduce potentially painful hot spots.

Reason 2: Hygiene. Keeping your pants clean is important. Let's just say underwear adds another barrier to help maintain that cleanliness.

Long underwear.
Similar to your long sleeve shirt, your bottom base layer is going to be what you sleep in and hang out in at camp. Wool or synthetic is just personal preference. I am a big fan of Minus 33 base layers. They have amazingly comfy long sleeve wool leggings to wear as thin pants at camp or an extra layer to hike in winter.

Hiking Shoes.
My vote for the most important piece of clothing. But, boots or trail runners? Let's settle this debate now.
- Boots. More durable, thicker tread and more reinforced structure. Therefore, they will last

longer on particularly rocky sections of the Trail like Pennsylvania. Many argue boots provide more ankle support as well. The BIG problem with boots is their breathability, or lack thereof. All of that extra protective material acts as a sponge for rainwater and mud which can take days to dry out. So what? Well, wet and tender feet means a higher probability of blisters, athlete's foot, moldy socks and all sorts of nasty stuff. With the AT being unavoidably wet, you should think twice before buying big, spongy boots.

- Trail Runners. Essentially running shoes with thicker tread. They are lightweight, breathable and dry fast. They are also much more comfortable than a stiff boot. Many trail runner advocates claim their ankles actually grow stronger in lieu of a boot's support. Trail runners can be more expensive though as you may demolish 3 or 4 pairs on your hike vs only 2 pairs of boots.

I hiked with a sort of half breed (Salewa Firetail) for most of the Trail. They were somewhere in between a lightweight boot and a heavyweight trail runner. They worked well and held up to the rockiest parts of Pennsylvania. However, I decided to switch to lightweight trail runners (Brooks Cascadia) towards the end. They were more like a running shoe than a hiking shoe. The feel of a trail running shoe was dramatically more comfortable. They were LIGHT and fluffy and oh, so comfy. Shall we call them foot pillows? My feet dried faster and, for the first time, were nearly blister free.

Switching from a heavy shoe to a light shoe was one of the most common gear switches on the Trail. There are a few, small rocky sections that might chew up your trail runners and make you wish you had thicker tread. For me though (and most), the comfort and blister free lifestyle of a trail runner is well worth going through an extra pair or two.

More than any other gear item, you need to try on your hiking shoes before buying them. All shoe companies have styles and cuts that may or may not work for YOUR feet. Keep in mind you may want to buy your shoes a half size up for two reasons: 1) your feet will swell slightly as you hike and 2) you will probably hike in thick socks and/ or additional sock liners.

If I were to hike the AT again, I'd go with a pair from Salomon. Models like XA Pro are as durable as a boot, but still as breathable as a trail runner. Their Speedcross is a lightweight trail runner with big teeth-like tread. Salomon shoes also have quick lace systems that make it effortless to tighten and loosen. Preferably no Goretex because it can trap water inside the shoe.

Keen is considered to be the best choice for boots - comfortable and durable. They also have a few lightweight options like the Versatrail that can be a great compromise.

2 Pairs of Socks.
Get wool socks that have some degree of compression. I prefer them to ride well above my ankle, even up to my shin. Beyond that, there are a lot of great brands out there. Darn Tough, Fits, Farm to Feet, Wigwam, and Injinji to name a few. Injinji's toe segmentation helps with blister prevention. Darn Tough is known for durability. Farm to Feet Socks and Fits Socks are my favorite. Both of these brands just feel quality.

Farm to Feet socks are 100% American made merino wool, have a comfortable level of compression and feel awesome on your feet. Their Damascus Crew model gets my vote.

Fits is a tough rival. Also American made and wool, Fits are extremely soft and have great color patterns. The comfortable contours of the compression on their Performance Trail socks make it another go to sock.

2 Pairs of Sock Liners.
Sock liners were something that I did not find in my pre-AT research. They are basically very thin socks designed to be worn underneath your main socks. I added liners (Smartwool) quickly into my hike and continued to hike in them until the last mile. They significantly reduced friction and blisters for me.

Camp Shoes.
After several hours of heavy pounding on roots and rocks and supporting your body and pack weight, your feet will be crying by the end of the day. More often than not, they will also be sweaty or still wet from a puddle you stepped in earlier. Exposing them to fresh air for a few hours is crucial and amazingly refreshing. I can remember getting so excited as I approached camp every night at the thought of my feet getting out of the sock-and-shoe steam room. Some things to consider with your camp shoes:

- Simple. These are not meant for hiking. Don't worry about support, lacing, etc.
- Breathable. A LOT of ventilation. Let those feet dry out.
- 100% Waterproof. Little or no possibility for absorption.
- Heel Cover. You may need to do a little walking in

your camp shoes. The water source could be a quarter mile away or down a hill. Maybe you are in town and want to stroll down to the laundromat while your hiking shoes dry. This can also be much more stable for fording rivers in. Some people use flip-flops. However, I want a heel cover or strap.

I hiked with Crocs. They were a little heavy (12 oz.), but worked well otherwise. There are several barefoot sandal companies to consider that weigh half as much. Xero Shoes are great and are what I would choose on my next hike. They are ultralight and minimal sandals complete with a heel strap. So light, you can roll them up in your pocket. I would feel comfortable crossing streams in them or hiking several miles in them. Some people actually run ultra-marathons in these things.

Insoles.
I used Superfeet. They were more durable than the shoe manufacturer's insole. Note that I have severe metatarsal issues and supplemented the insole with padding. Almost every hiker I knew encountered some sort of foot injury or problem. Sometimes the toe box was too tight or the lacing too loose or the arch support was too high. I would highly recommend checking in with a podiatrist before heading out to see what issues you might encounter.

Gaiters.
Thick gaiters are unnecessary. Your feet will get wet no matter what and your ankles can handle grazing the brush without them. I ended up wearing some very light gaiters (Dirty Girl) about halfway through the Trail. They were an annoying addition to your feet and force you to attach a

Velcro strap to the heel of your shoes. However, they helped prevent small pebbles and pine straw from getting into my shoes. Without the gaiters, I was stopping every mile or two to empty out debris which made the hassle of gaiters well worth it.

Winter Additions.

2 (more) Long Sleeve Shirts.
I still slept in my other long sleeve shirt mentioned above. Snowy days called for more warmth while hiking. I added a thick, long sleeve wool shirt (Minus 33) as well as a thin synthetic base layer from Walmart. I got rid of one of my tshirts. I still wear my thick Minus 33 wool base layer around and loved how warm, comfortable and quality the stitching is. Get one.

Beanie.
A wool beanie is an important addition to insulate your head. I would double up the beanie (Arc'teryx) and my Buff while sleeping.

2 Pairs of Gloves.
Same layering principle. I had one pair of gloves act as a tough, wind resistant shell. This shell was fingertip-less which was a nice option itself on more moderate winter days. Make sure this pair has a strong grip and is not prone to slip on your trekking pole handles.

The other pair, while still gloves, acted as a liner. They were wool and helped insulate as a base layer. While this combination did work for me, there were several especially cold days that I had to put the cold metal trekking poles away and tuck my hands under my armpits while I hiked. Burrrrrr.

Camp Socks.
Made for sleeping, not hiking. My feet could get frigidly numb on winter nights. I added an extra pair of irregularly thick wool socks to sleep in.

Female Items.
(Males jump ahead to pg. 163)

Again, I asked AT (and PCT and AZT!) record holder, Heather 'Anish' Anderson (http://facebook.com/AnishHikes) to help you ladies out in this section.

-Heather starts writing here -

Sports Bras.
Finding the right bra for long distance hiking can be a daunting task. Like shoes, fit is individualized and there are so many shapes and sizes to accommodate. There is no perfect bra that will work for every woman! It's great to ask in forums or other hikers what their favorites are, but keep in mind who you're talking to. What works for an A-cup won't necessarily work for a D-cup and vice versa. Also, a bra that works great on the PCT may not wick well enough on the AT.

Here are some basic factors to consider:
The AT is wet: high humidity and lots of rain, all the time. The right sports bra will dry quickly to avoid chafing. Soak the bra you intend to wear, wring it out and hang it

up to dry. Time how long it takes. If you have several candidates, do a side by side comparison.

Backpacking is a low-medium impact sport. You won't need a bra that smashes you down uncomfortably. Remember, you will be wearing this all day long. You'll want adequate support that is also comfortable and allows you to breathe.

Look for wide straps that don't cut into your neck. Also watch for seams that might cause sores or chafing under the shoulder strap of your pack.

I hiked with a cheap sports bra on my first AT thru-hike and it never dried. It was miserable. The second time I wore a bikini top, which dried instantly, but it dug into my neck. More recently I've been wearing the merino wool Balance Bralette by Ibex or the spandex Sports Bras by BSkinz. Both of these have been superior. For women who are a size D or more, many people I've met recommend the Fiona or Juno by Moving Comfort or the PhD Seamless bra by Smartwool if you prefer merino.

Underwear.
As with a bra, you'll want underwear that is comfortable and dries quickly. Synthetic fabrics often retain odors and harbor bacterial growth. Merino wool is an excellent alternative. Never use cotton since it's long dry time can lead to chafing as well as an environment where bacteria can multiply rapidly. Many women also opt to wear no undergarments at all. This provides maximum ventilation, but may lead to chafing or just be too odd or uncomfortable for you. However, even if you wear undergarments, removing them at break time can help

keep you comfortable and help avoid bacterial build-up.

Rinsing underwear out daily (always away from water sources) and allowing one pair to dry while you wear another one is the ideal way to keep the risk of an infection (as well as odor) down. If you're uncomfortable with hanging your undies on the outside of your pack to dry, its fine to wait to wash them in town as long as it's at least once every 2-3 wears.

In short, wash up daily with either soap and water, plain water, or a non-antibacterial wipe. Wear comfortable undergarments that dry quickly and don't foster bacterial growth. Wash them regularly as well. Manage your period with the products you feel most comfortable with that also suit your own personal flow and medical history. Stay hydrated and keep your kidneys flushed to avoid a UTI. Most importantly, relax and enjoy hiking!

-Heather ends writing here -

CHAPTER 11

Food and Nutrition

The Caloric Feast.

A thru-hiker's appetite is the stuff of myth and legend. You are about to become a human trash can. Just warn friends and family to keep their fingers and toes away from your mouth.

You are about to burn A LOT of calories. Most thru-hikers cannot consume enough calories to keep up with their rate of depletion and end up losing some, if not a lot of, weight.

I am 5'10 and started at 165 lbs. (comfortably skinny dude). I finished around 155 lbs. (uncomfortably skinny dude). I aimed to eat at least 4,000 calories a day on the Trail and 8,000 calories a day in town.

I know… it sounds crazy. It's not.

Your body weight, intensity of hiking, sex and pack weight all affect how many calories you burn per hour.

The burn rate estimates range from 300 calories an hour for a 110 pound female up to 700 calories per hour for 220 pound male. It is not uncommon for hikers to consume 6,000 calories on long, intense days of hiking.

In town, I would typically eat a pizza (yea a big, fat one), followed by a salad, a pint of Ben and Jerry's Chocolate Fudge Brownie ice cream, a banana, a pint of strawberries and finally, a cold beer (or two). The next morning would be yogurt, an orange, a pint of blueberries, eggs, bacon and pancakes. Note the emphasis on two things in town: 1) Fresh foods like salad and fruit and 2) high calorie 'junk'. I remember sitting in hotel rooms tallying up nutrition labels competing to see if any of us had broken 10,000 calories.

I loved the appetite. Sure, there were times I might have gone overboard and approached a food induced coma. However, there has been no other time in my life that I could eat, and enjoy eating, as much food as I did on my thru-hike. Totally guilt free fat ass mode.

The best backpacking food is...

Packable.
Keep in mind you will toss around, unload and repack all of your trail food... a lot. This is where puffy bread, brittle crackers and squishy fruits become impractical. Keep it compact and durable.

Easy.
Minimal (or no) cooking and minimal (or no) cleanup. You want to be able to drop your bag, unzip a pocket and eat.

Setting up the pots and stove, waiting for the food to cook and then cleaning everything up takes time and effort.

Many ultra-light distance hikers opt to leave the stove behind entirely and go for a "non-cook meal plan". I loved a hot meal at the end of the day though. I recommend a compromise - only cook one meal a day, dinner. It's the end of the day so you have time to bust out the stove and chill. A hot meal, particularly in winter will be your guardian angel.

Lightweight.
To a certain degree, density is the ultimate goal (i.e. high calorie-to-oz. ratio). I typically only carry food that is at least 100 calories per oz. Your back and knees will appreciate every extra ounce you can shave off. You want "waterless" or dehydrated food.

Tasty.
Don't torture yourself out there. Six months of noodles just ain't gonna cut it. Try to mix up your food and flavors as much as possible. Be sure to pack yourself a treat or two to look forward to everyday. I specifically craved sugar and salt on the Trail. A constant supply of Mike and Ikes (fruity candy) kept me sane. I can remember have mini meditation sessions as I suckled each piece in my mouth. Find your 'Mike and Ikes'.

High in Nutrition.
Your body is burning up energy at an alarming rate. Make sure your food packs in quality nutrition to keep up with this burn rate. Don't stress about tallying all of these amounts up at every resupply. Just know that you are backpacking for a long time and pushing your body more

than you probably ever have. Checking on these nutrients can keep you healthy - specifically prevent skin issues, muscles cramps, stress fractures and exhaustion.

The FDA recommended daily amounts are listed below. You should be sure to get at least this much on the Trail.

- Carbohydrates (300 g). Simple carbs are fast-burning fuel from sugar: candy, corn syrup, and soda, for example. Complex carbs and starches are slow-burning fuel found in fiber-rich food like oatmeal, brown rice, and green vegetables. You want a combination of both simple and complex carbs.
- Fats (65 g). The most calorie-dense food and the best for keeping your pack weight low. Fats help absorb vitamins and provide a great long term storage of energy.
- Protein (50 g). Protein helps repair damaged tissue as well as build new tissue. Your muscles need it.
- Fiber (25 g). When you are out on the Trail consuming large volumes of food - fiber is there to regulate your digestive tract. Fiber also helps regulate and maintain your blood sugar levels which can be crucial in controlling simple sugar spikes and crashes.
- Electrolytes. You are going to sweat a lot and need a lot of electrolytes. There are 7 major electrolytes. I focus on sodium (2,400 mg), potassium (4,500 mg) and calcium (1,000 mg). These help control water levels and, when depleted, can cause cramping and muscle weakness.
- Vitamins: Vitamin C (60 mg), Vitamin E (30 IU), Vitamin A (5,000 IU), Iron (18 mg).

How Much Food Should I Carry?

You won't be foraging for nuts and berries nor hunting birds and rabbits. You will resupply all food in town and carry all of it in your pack. The distance between towns can range anywhere from 40 to 100 miles or about 3 to 7 days.

Rationing food properly can be a delicate balancing act. You don't want to over pack extra pounds of food. But, it would be horrible and somewhat dangerous, to under pack and run out of food.

Let's say your next trail town is 75 miles away. You plan to average 15 miles per day. Therefore, you need 5 days' worth of food. At the grocery store, I always think on a per-meal-basis. So plan 5 breakfasts, 5 lunches, 5 dinners and then any daily 'extras' (snacks, desserts, drinks).

Typically you want 1.5 to 2 lbs. of food per day. If you are not sure how much you need for a meal (the small packet of tuna or the big one?), use this weight range for some rough guidance.

Pack your food bag at the top of your pack... especially the smashable or leakable items. This will also make it easy to access whenever you stop in the day. Things like sleeping bag, pad, clothes, and stove should be at the bottom. I always made sure to strategically scatter my food in easy access spots, like my hip-belt pockets so I could hike AND eat.

31 Food Ideas.

1. Oatmeal Packets. A backpacking food staple. The best thing about these packets is that they serve as a bowl. Just add hot water to heat the oats inside. Get variety packs.

2. Grits. You don't have to be Southern to love grits. As easy as oatmeal and can be a nice addition to mix up your breakfast options.

3. Greenbelly Meal. As the founder, I am biased. I developed the recipe with a food scientist and chef, tested the flavor profiles relentlessly with other hikers, and made sure the final product met my original goal - create the best backpacking meal on the planet. Each meal pouch provides high levels of balanced nutrition (like 33% of your DV down the label) using fresh, all-natural ingredients. They are ready-to-eat meal bars that taste heavenly (www.greenbelly.co).

4. Dried Fruits. Fresh fruit is generally too heavy and delicate. Dried fruit provides dense sugar which can be a healthier alternative to candy.

5. Nuts and Seeds. Calories! Salted, roasted, whatever. Nuts are a tasty way to pack in dense calories, protein and healthy fats and oils. Peanuts, cashews, sunflower seeds, almonds, pecans, pistachios, walnuts and pumpkin seeds to name a few.

6. Powder Meals. There are a ton of 'powder' options out there. From complete meal replacements to weight lifting supplements. Aim to keep it minimally processed.

7. Meats. Beef jerky, salami and tuna are my favorite non-cook meats for the trail. None of them need refrigeration. All of them are tasty and high in protein and sodium. The New Primal makes my favorite beef jerky. Think of them like "quality Slim Jims". They also come in a huge variety of flavors.

8. Cheese. Cheese can be a heavy food for some ultralight backpackers. However, it can pack in a lot of calories and fat. Not to mention, it can really enhance the meat flavor. Aim for 'harder' cheeses - they are more shelf stable.

9. Tortillas or Pita. Bread can be too bulky and fluffy for backpacking. Tortillas are compact and can take a beating. Great for wraps.

10. Bagels. If tortillas are too flat, bagels can help provide that nice fluffy texture of bread.

11. Crackers. High in carbohydrates and sodium. Hang them on the outside of your pack with a bandanna if you think they'll get smashed inside.

12. Instant Noodles. Get noodles instead of pasta. Seasoned noodles generally don't need a lot of cleanup compared to creamy pastas which can leave your bowl or cup a sticky mess. They also have a lot of carbohydrates.

13. Instant Rice. A great base for a backpacking dinner meal. There are countless rice varieties with different seasonings and veggie fixin's at the store.

14. Couscous. Cooks in 5 minutes - much faster than rice or noodles. The light texture can be a nice dinner relief.

High in fiber. A little less filling in my opinion.

15. Instant Potatoes. Another backpacking staple and great meal base. Ultralight backpacking food with carbs and sodium.

16. Dried Veggies. It is hard to eat veggies on the trail. Dried peas, carrots, corns, etc are an exception.

17. Lentils. I had not ever eaten this until the AT. In the legume family (with peanuts and peas), Lentils are an ancient superfood rich in calories, protein, fiber and Iron. Takes a few extra minutes to cook.

18. Freeze Dried Meals. Add hot water, stir, seal and then wait a few minutes. Plenty of options of flavors, recipes and brands to choose from for dinner.

19. Chews and Gels. Chews have a gummy/ candy-like consistency. Goos and gels have a honey-like consistency. All can range in what they aim to provide - caffeine, electrolytes, etc.

20. Peanut or Almond Butter (or Nutella). The king of backpacking food. Crammed with calories, fat, sodium and protein. Ready-to-eat and can lather on almost anything.

21. Honey. Let peanut butter be the food of choice for the savory loving backpacking community. But, give the sweet award to honey. Sweeten up tea, crackers or eat it straight.

22. Granola Bar. Too many options to name. There are

protein bars, energy bars, snack bars, nutrition bars, food bars - you name it. Ready-to-eat and usually high in nutrition.

23. Hummus. A lesser known backpacking superfood. On top of the yummy taste, hummus has dense calories, carbs, protein and fiber.

24. Drink Tabs. Great source for electrolytes and enhances hydration. Drop a tab in your water and watch it fizz away (like Alka-Seltzer).

25. Drink Powder Mixes. Similar benefits as the tabs. Usually with a lot more flavor options and some have vitamin and mineral enhancements.

26. Hot Drink- Tea, Coffee, Hot Chocolate, Cider. I drank instant coffee in the morning and tea at night. In particular, chamomile tea before bed was a nice way to end the day.

27. Multivitamin. Get those vitamins and minerals without the bulky food. Particularly good to get your Vitamin C and Calcium which are less easy to come by in shelf stable trail food.

28. Fruit Powders. Another hidden backpacking food gem. Pour fruit powder into an ounce of water and take a healthy fruit drink shot. Great way to get some fruit nutrition without the weight.

29. Olive Oil. Super dense calories and fat. It can add some much needed moisture to a dry noodle or rice dish... crackers and tuna as well. A little 5 oz. bottle will do. Pack

in an isolated bag in case it busts.

30. Spices - salt, pepper, garlic, chili. Keep your carb dinners (noodle, rice, couscous, potatoes) plain and spice it up to your liking with a DIY seasoning kit. Portion it into smaller ziploc bags to save weight.

31. Seaweed. Ultra-lightweight, chock full of vitamins and minerals, and lasts a looong time. You can throw it in a soup or eat it raw as a snack.

18 Simple Meals (4 ingredients or less).

Some thru-hikers would probably prefer to get their meals through a feeding tube than prep and cook. Others take pride in their gourmet meal plans and experimental recipes. Here are just some ideas to get your appetite going.

1. Concoction. Carnation Instant Breakfast Mix + Brownie Mix + Oats + Instant Coffee Powder. My favorite breakfast. Mix it all up into one, secure bag. Eyeball your portion each morning into a cup and add cold water. Mix it and sluuuurp it up.

2. Bacon and Eggs. Bacon Bits + Mashed Potatoes + Powdered Eggs. I recommend keeping the eggs separate. I saw people eat this. But, the powdered eggs were just not for me.

3. Cereal. Dried Fruit + Powdered Milk + Cereal/ Granola. Powdered milk is shelf stable and provides a lightweight source of calcium. Just add water. Chewy dried fruits like

apricots and cranberries and blueberries work best.

4. Salmon Bagel. Salmon + Bagel + Cream Cheese. A simple breakfast sandwich that doesn't require any heat, but still provides a tasty protein and carb boost. Single-use cream cheese packets can be found at breakfast and many coffee shops. There are some great ready-to-eat salmon packets (SeaBear) as well.

5. Oatmeal. Nuts + Oatmeal + Raisins. These three ingredients are backpacking staples for good reason. Accessible, easy to prepare and nutritious.

6. Nutella Wrap. Tortilla + Nutella + Banana Chips. An easy wrap. Nutella (available in pouches) is essentially a sweet and chocolaty version of peanut butter. Banana chips or peanuts give it a nice crunch.

7. Picnic. Crackers + Cheese + Meat. Cured, salty meat. Yes, please.

8. Pita Wrap. Fresh Veggies + Pita Bread + Hummus. Pita bread is nearly as pack-friendly as tortillas. Cucumbers and red peppers pack reasonably well.

9. Pizza Wrap. Tortillas + Tomato Sauce + Cheese + Pepperoni. Other than packing it out, this is as close as you'll get to pizza on the Trail.

10. Meat and Potatoes. Pre-cooked Sausage + Mashed Potatoes + Chives. One of my most common meals. Found at almost any grocery store and super simple.

11. Chicken Couscous. Couscous + Cheese + Chicken +

Dried Veggies.

12. Cashew Noodle. Noodles + Curry Paste + Dried Veggies + Cashews. For the vegetarians, curry powder (or a smidge of paste) can be mixed with cashews and any veggies on hand.

13. Thai Curry. Rice + Tuna + Coconut Milk + Yellow Curry. Powdered coconut milk and yellow curry pastes/ powders can be found in the international food section of the supermarket.

14. Burrito. Taco Mix + Tortillas + Rice + Black Beans.

15. Jerky Noodle. Noodles + Soy Sauce + Beef Jerky.

16. Trail Mix on Steroids. Honey + Peanut Butter + Trail Mix. I remember pouring my trail mix into my half eaten peanut butter jar, squeezing a mound of honey inside and stirring. A filling glob of sweet and salty.

17. Chili Mac. Macaroni Noodle + Red Beans + Chili Mix + Cheese.

18. Tuna Alfredo. Noodles + Pesto/ Alfredo + Olive Oil + Tuna. Pesto and/ or Alfredo sauce comes in powdered forms and is another excellent lightweight flavor option for the Trail.

Coffee.

Just behind Mike and Ike's, coffee was a close second for my favorite treat. In the summer, I never cooked in the morning. In winter, I was happy to spend a few extra minutes to have a hot cup of coffee. The average 8 oz. cup of coffee contains 100mg of caffeine which, as you know, can be an awesome energy boost to start the day. That boost was crucial on some snowy, sluggish mornings.

You won't be able to pack out the beloved Keurig for an easy cup of joe. On the AT, I learned just how far people will go for a good cup of coffee though. Let's go over the main brewing options. Note I am no coffee connoisseur.

Instant Coffee.
The most popular option. These just-add-water coffee crystal packs are the easiest and lightest way to get your coffee fix on the trail. Walmart has drinkable options. I personally enjoyed Starbucks packs the most. Price varies a lot with quality.

French Press.
I find that the French press makes the most quality cup of coffee. French press is the messiest and heaviest option though. The actual press has to fit your cup perfectly too. This means you usually need to buy the cup and press together as a set. Combined they should weigh about 7 oz.

Drip Cones (with a disposable filter).
Makes a good tasting cup of coffee. Set this cone on top of your cup or mug. Stack on a regular disposable paper filter. Add in coffee grounds. Pour hot water onto coffee ground and let it slowly drip into the cup. The cone should weigh about 2.5 oz. Don't forget to pack out the paper filter.

Reusable Filter.
Same as the drip cone except without the trash. You will, however, have to clean out the filter instead of just throwing it away.

Cowboy Coffee (aka 'mud').
What do you do when you are on the AT with coffee grounds and no filter? Cowboy it! Pour the grounds directly into your cup or mug and just add hot water. You can drink the grounds or filter them out with your teeth. Definitely a stronger brew.

CHAPTER 12

Water and Hydration

One of my favorite things about hiking the Appalachian Trail was drinking the natural water. Yummy. There is something awesomely primal about drinking directly from the source - somewhat on par with foraging or hunting for your meal (or wrestling a bear or pounding your chest from a mountain top). Depending on what elements are present, you can often taste the subtle differences in the water. It is usually refreshingly cold as well. Okay, enough.

Proper hydration is just as important as proper nutrition. You need to know how to stay fueled AND hydrated.

How much water should I carry?

"Drink 8 glasses of water" or nearly 2 liters is the classic rule of thumb for everyday life. As you can imagine though, the Trail requires a lot more physical exertion than everyday life and, subsequently, a lot more water.

How much water you should carry varies from person to

person. Body weight, pack weight, gender, terrain difficulty, speed, temperature and altitude all affect your hydration needs. Some thru-hikers carry at least 2 liters of water at all times. Some don't carry any - electing to only drink at the water sources. I typically carried about a liter of water with me. Keep in mind a few things about hydrating on the AT:

Water is Darn Heavy.
Over 2 lbs. per liter. Considering you will only carry about 2 lbs. of food per day, water can add a relatively huge amount of weight to your pack. Think twice before loading up on several liters.

Drink Before Setting Off (or 'Camel Up').
I usually aimed to sip down a liter anytime I was leaving a water source. This meant during breakfast at the shelter, heading to the trailhead from town, or just before leaving the stream where I had stopped for lunch. Avoid chugging if you can as it'll pass through you quicker.

Listen to Your Body.
In more extreme temperatures, hydration was almost a constant flow, drinking every few minutes. On one particularly hot and humid summer day in New York, I pushed over 20 miles and was sweating buckets. Every inch was drenched in sweat. It looked like I had just gone for a fully-clothed swim in a pool.

I remember drinking 8 liters of water that day and still feeling light headed from dehydration that evening. My body was telling me it needed more water… and probably more electrolytes. I could not believe that over 2 gallons had still not been enough to hydrate me.

Don't let winter fool you either. Fluids are constantly being depleted no matter how low the temperature. While I get lightheaded, a lot of hikers get muscle cramps when dehydrated. Be aware of what your body is telling you.

Monitor Your Urine.
An easy way to gauge your hydration level is by monitoring the color of your urine. Dark yellow means you are under hydrated. Clear means you are over hydrated. I always aimed for a slightly yellow tint and hoped to err on the overhydrated side. Okay, who wants to talk more about their urine color?

Plan Your Water Sources Every Morning.
I checked my AWOL guide every morning to see where the water sources would be and planned my snack and meal breaks accordingly. You will quickly learn how much water your body needs to get 5, 10, 15 miles down trail.

Water Abundance.
Fortunately, water is readily available all along the AT. You practically hike *through* it in Maine. Most sections have sources strung along every 2-8 miles. There were a few days in Pennsylvania where I loaded up with over 2 liters of water because the sources were more like 15 miles apart. Note there are 'seasonal sources'. These can be bone dry in less rainy parts of the year. They are not very common though and can be easily planned around.

Where will I fill up my water?

Sometimes a backyard may be nearby and someone has

posted a sign directing you to use their hose. Most of the time you will fill up from natural sources like a pond or a stream.

Flowing Sources (Streams, Springs and Rivers).
Generally a bit cleaner and has naturally already filtered out the 'floaties'. Floaties can be any sort of particle that makes the water murky - leaves, algae, bugs, etc. Flowing water is easier to fill a container from... particularly collapsible bottles that need the pressure from the flow to expand and open as they fill.

Stagnant Sources (Ponds, Lakes, Puddles).
If it is visibly dirty, use a bandanna or camp towel to filter out the floaties before letting them clog up your water filter. Some ponds are also too shallow to completely submerge your container in. You may need a firm cup to scoop up water little by little.

Shelters.
Most shelters have some sort of water source (flowing or stagnant) nearby within 1/10 of a mile. Some shelters actually have a convenient PVC pipe channeling the source out of the ground from a nearby spring.

Town.
Take advantage of the easy water in town before hitting the Trail again.

Where should I store my water?

I used two containers - 1 plastic bottle for my dirty water and 1 collapsible bottle for my clean water. I recommend 1 liter capacity for your clean water and 2 liter capacity for your dirty water. This allows you to fill up more than enough dirty water and keep hiking. You can always filter it later when you get to a good resting point.

Plastic Bottle.
I recommend recycled plastic bottles. They are everywhere and can be replaced easily. My Smart Water bottle was super durable and lasted over 2,000 miles (and I still have it!). Most water bottles in the store are heavy and very stiff making them slightly bulkier and less malleable in your pack. In this case, I think cheaper is better.

Collapsible Bottle.
These collapse and fold and are very light. When they are empty, they conveniently roll up and can be tucked away in your pack. Collapsible bottles are generally less durable. My Platypus popped when I accidentally dropped it on a rock. I liked it enough though and bought another one in the next trail town.

Bladder/ Reservoir.
Like a collapsible bottle with a hose and mouthpiece. The bladder usually tucks inside the back wall of your pack. The hose snakes out around your shoulder with the mouthpiece resting a few inches from your mouth. The advantage is that you can suck water through the hose and hydrate as you hike. They are heavy though and can be a pain to clean. I also did not like not being able to visualize how much I was drinking. By seeing my bottle every time I drank, I was able to easily ration my dwindling supply before reaching the next water source.

Should I treat my water?

Ahh, if only we could just dip our bottle into the fresh mountain streams and chug away. Unfortunately, it ain't quite like that. That yummy crystal clean spring could contain microscopic parasites and put you off the Trail for a few weeks with diarrhea... or worse.

Note there are plenty of clean water sources on the Trail. In fact, the vast majority of them are clean and perfectly fine to drink from. I honestly don't know if I heard of anyone with a *confirmed* case of Giardia. If someone had Diarrhea, there were always other variables that could have been the culprit.

I must admit by the end of the Trail, I quit treating most of my water altogether. The air was below freezing and stopping to filter water meant taking off my gloves and exposing my numb fingers to icy water. I couldn't be bothered. Scooping and chugging was just too easy.

However, you have no way of knowing what is safe to drink untreated. It only takes two minutes to treat your water and you only fill up a few times a day. The small chance you do catch something could be horrible. Always treat your water because the risk is just not worth it.

How should I treat my water?

Every water purification has its advantages and disadvantages. But, most remove Giardia and Cryptosporidium, which are common parasites in water unseen to the naked eye. Let's dig into your options to clean water.

Filters.

The most common method used on the AT. Dirty water flows through a high tech filter which removes all the nasty stuff. Clean water comes out the other end.

- Squeeze. Sawyer Squeeze is what I used and would use again. It is a small nozzle that screws on top of your water container. The threads match most water bottles (Smart Water bottles namely) as well as most water bladders, including the bladders Sawyer provides with the filter. It is easy to use and lightweight. The one downside is that it is slower than a pump. I would not want to wait and manually squeeze several liters of water through one.

- Gravity. Two bags connected by a hose with the filter. You fill one bag with dirty water and hang it higher than the other bag. The dirty water will flow through the hose and filter into the other clean water bag. Some people love being able to scoop up water, let gravity do the work and come back to a clean bag. In my opinion, they are too bulky and impractical while filling up in the day though.

- Pump. Similar to the squeeze, except you utilize the pump mechanism to flow the water through the filter faster. You stick one end of the chord into the water source and pump clean water out the other end. The big advantage is the ability to quickly filter larger volumes of water. If you are hiking with a partner, this may be a good option. As a solo hiker though, waiting an extra 30 seconds to squeeze out my liter was not an issue. I also don't like all of the moving parts in a pump which seem to be a pain to clean as well as increase the likelihood of malfunction.

Boiling.
You already have a stove, so why bring anything else for treatment? Leaving the filter behind and boiling water with your stove (or fire) can certainly save weight. I drank my fair share of boiled water on the Trail. It was mainly only leftover from cooking though.

Boiling water several times a day is extremely impractical. Your cup or pot is not big enough to boil a liter or two of water. You will have to boil several cups before having enough to hit the trail and waste a lot of fuel in the meantime. Filling up mid-day is even more annoying. Pull out the stove, wait for the water to boil, and then wait for it to cool down enough to be drinkable. In short, boiling water = no fun.

UV Light.
Some treatment devices, like SteriPEN, utilize UV light to electronically 'zap' and kill the nasty stuff. You dip the pen into your water container, turn on the light bulb and wait a minute or two. These seem easy enough. However, they operate on batteries which can die any moment. That means managing and carrying around spares. The pen does not filter out any floaties either. You will have to go an extra effort to eliminate them... or you end up just drinking them.

Chemicals.
Not quite as common as filters, but still very common on the AT. These are lighter than filters, require much less

effort and are inexpensive. You put a few drops into dirty water, shake it up and wait 30 minutes for the chemicals to kill everything. There are two main chemical drops or tablets to choose from: 1) Chlorine Dioxide and 2) Iodine. Iodine leaves the water tasting strange and is commonly used with flavor neutralizing tablets.

I did not use chemicals because they are consumable and can be depleted. Gas stations and grocery stores do not carry them either meaning you have to mail drop them or stock up at an outfitter. That minimum 30 minute wait sounds inconvenient as well. Not to mention, these are in fact *chemicals*.

CHAPTER 13

Dangers

I feel like one of the most common questions thru-hikers get asked is *"Is it dangerous?"* Maybe we fear the unknown or maybe pop culture has portrayed the woods to be full of ravenous bears and estranged murderers.

Basically, the AT is very safe. I certainly experienced several of the 'dangers' listed below. But how dangerous is a sprained ankle or poison ivy? I never experienced anything nor knew anyone who experienced anything life threatening. No bear attacks, snake bites, murders, what have you.

Out of hundreds of hikers, I knew ONE person who had gotten Lyme Disease. He felt flu-like symptoms for several days before seeing a doctor in town. The doctor gave him antibiotics for a few weeks and he had a full recovery.

I am not trying to lighten the severity of Lyme Disease nor any other potential dangers. However, keep things in perspective. I feel more safe on the AT than, say, driving at 70 miles per hour down the interstate. Real danger is highly improbable and even less so with some caution.

Wildlife.

Black Bears.
Remember, these are much smaller than the big carnivorous Grizzlies out West. You'll see plenty of Black Bears. I'd guess I saw about 25 total. Just let 'em be. They are probably much more afraid of you than you are of them. Always bear bag, especially in the 'dense' sections like New Jersey and around The Smoky's. I never hiked with a bear canister or bear spray.

Bear Bag 101; Find a sturdy limb about 20 feet off the ground. Tie something with weight to one end of your paracord (rock, limb, etc.) and your food bag to the other. Hurl the weighted end over the limb and pull your bag up. Tie it off. The goal is to keep the bag out of reach from the tree, the limbs and the ground. Therefore, make sure it is hanging several feet below the limb, several feet away from the tree column and at least 15 feet off the ground.

Black Flies and Mosquitoes.
Yes, they suck. As a SOBO, the black flies in Maine were the stuff of nightmares. I literally ran from them at times. Even on some hot and sweaty days, I would armor every inch of exposed skin with some sort clothing. Wear repellent, stand near a smoky fire or use your clothes to cover up more.

Coyotes.
Meh. Uncommon and skittish.

Mice.
Yes, they are in some shelters and *can* carry diseases. As

mentioned though, just keep your food hung or well attended and they won't bother you much.

Poison Ivy.

Very common. Vines with green leaves of three. Avoid it at all costs. Skin contact causes heavy itching for most people. Hike in pants or mid-calf socks. Wash up as soon as possible before it spreads to other parts of your body. I had one very uncomfortable encounter on my ankles. I bought some calamine lotion in town and the itching slowed after a few days.

Snakes.

By far the most common snake I saw were harmless 1 foot Garter snakes. I saw a lot of 3-4 foot Black Racers and Rat Snakes as well. The only venomous snakes on the AT are Copperheads and Rattlesnakes. There is a slim chance of encountering a Water Moccasin (cottonmouth) in low elevation and only in the most Southern states.

Don't hike with both headphones in and music blaring. While I only saw a few rattlesnakes, one of them was a very close encounter. It was coiled up, tail rattling furiously, and poised to strike. I had stopped to drink some water and stepped way too close to this guy. I cautiously moved back and, thankfully, he never struck. If you do plan on using headphones, it might be a good idea to only hike with one ear in at a time.

Spiders.

Brown Recluse and Black Widow are the two. They like dry wood piles so keep your eyes peeled when digging for fire wood.

Ticks.
I only got a few tick bites. They can carry Lyme Disease
though. Wear repellent, especially in tight places like your
socks and underwear line. Give yourself a "tick check" as
often as possible. Be sure not to leave the head of the tick
embedded in your skin when removing.

Weather.

Cold.
Depending on when you leave, you may or may not
encounter snow. Snow is relatively 'dry' and can be
brushed off. Cold rain is much more difficult to manage.
Inevitable, your feet will get wet and probably your pants
and legs as well. Long term exposure to cold rain can lead
to hypothermia. Be sure to carry more than enough warm
layers and keep your sleeping bag dry. Worst case, you
can always pull off the trail, setup camp and get into your
dry change of clothes and sleeping bag.

Hot.
Dehydration and heat exhaustion. Keep fluids flowing as
much as possible, especially in the hotter months. You
might encounter some 100 degree days that dehydrate you
even faster. Be sure to check your urine is a transparent
yellow color.

Storms.
Lightning storms, particularly on balds, can be dangerous.
I encountered a couple storms that made me think twice
before setting up on exposed mountain tops again. Here is
an entry from my journal about Avery Peak:

*I decided to stealth camp on the peak that night in hopes to catch
the sunrise. Being at that high of elevation, I knew it would be
risky with the volatile weather. I woke up rolled on the side wall
of my tent with my stakes popped out. My body was the only
thing keeping the tent grounded. The wind and lightning had
picked up so dramatically that I had to break camp and hike
down at 3 AM.*

People.

Hikers.
Just like anywhere, there can be some bad apples. Try to
stay with a group. Use the hitchhike safety tips from
earlier. In the rare instance you do encounter a bad apple,
they will more likely be from nearby town and not thru-
hikers.

A few buddies and I had an entertaining, and somewhat
scary encounter at a shelter in Pennsylvania. A couple had
been living there for nearly a week and were drunkenly
yelling at each other when we arrived… presumably on
some sort of drugs as well. Concerning and obnoxious to
say the least. It was pouring rain though and we did not
have much of an option but to stay put at the shelter. They
were not aggressive toward us at all. However, I was
definitely happy to have some buddies with me.

Hunters.
Hunting is permitted in some sections of the Trail. In these
sections, you need to wear a bright piece of orange
clothing. Keep it visible at all times (ideally on your head
or your chest). You'd hate to be mistaken for a buck (or a
turkey for that matter).

Injury.

Blisters.
Extremely common. Use your first aid kit (Vaseline, bandaids, duct tape) to reduce hot spots and treat existing ones. Toe socks can help reduce friction. You may need to adjust your shoes some.

Scrapes, Cuts and Gashes.
I never had anything more than minor cuts and scrapes - certainly no deep 'gashes' or scar-like wounds. I carried a small antiseptic wipe to clean the wound and then would put a bandaid on top to prevent it from further exposure.

Aches, Pains and Swelling.
You can use the "R.I.C.E" framework on particularly sore body parts. Rest, Ice, Compress and Elevate. Rest in town for an extra day or two. Ice it up. Use an Ace wrap to compress it without cutting off circulation. Prop it up so it is elevated above your heart.

The morning after a long day of hiking was always a rude awakening... literally. All sorts of body parts, particularly my feet, would be extremely achy. I found massaging my feet, arching my back out of the 'hiker hunch' and stretching my legs every morning to be helpful.

Fording Rivers.
You will need to cross over and hike directly through a lot of water. Bogs, streams and rivers. The rivers are the most dangerous. Most rivers flowing above your ankles will have some sort of foot bridge or line to hold on to as you walk through them. The Kennebec River is too deep and

actually has a volunteer to shuttle hikers across in a canoe (so cool). The footbridges can be slick so use those trekking poles if need be.

For fording, I always scoped out my route across before ever even leaving the bank. I'd much rather wade through steady shallow water than try to 'rock hop' around some rapids. Loosen your pack and unbuckle your sternum strap. If you were to fall, you would not want your bag to pull you down.

Some people would actually wade through buck naked. They did not want to risk wet clothes... and clothes can add a lot of resistance to the river flow. I'll let you decide though.

Sanitation.
As discussed in the water chapter, always treat your water. No one wants a couple weeks of diarrhea. Be sure to use hand sanitizer religiously.

Lost.
The Trail is well marked and you don't need a map. There were plenty of times though that the Trail crossed with another trail or was buried in thick leaves and I wandered a little off. You do need to be aware of the blazes and how long ago you last saw one. They should not be more than 100 yards apart.

If You Get Lost...
I use the 'satellite method'. You use your current location as a docking station to scope out potential directions the trail could be. This prevents you from wandering deeper into the woods and getting more lost.

1. Stop and mark your current location. Tie up something bright in a highly visible spot - maybe your orange camp towel on an elevated tree branch.
2. Walk in the direction you think the Trail is… never out of sight from that marker.
3. If you do not find the AT, go back to your marker and try another direction.
4. If you still cannot find it, establish a larger perimeter with more markers and repeat until you find the trail.

CHAPTER 14

Rehabilitation Phase

OMG, you finished your thru-hike!
Congrats. You're awesome. Soak in the accomplishment.
All of your early doubts have now transformed into
confidence and balls of steel. Yay, yay, yay.

Back Home.
Okay, now what?

Someone told me that leaving the AT was similar to how
they felt after being a war veteran. Nothing to do with the
trauma, rather the change in lifestyle and expectations.
Somewhat of a culture shock.

When I got back to my parent's house in Georgia on
December 18th, things were different. My hiking partner
and I sat in the living room and played with a puzzle for
hours... not talking much. It felt strange not hiking,
wearing blue jeans, sitting inside with a cleanly shaven
face and eating a wide variety of food.

A few days later, 17 of my family members packed out the
house to celebrate Christmas. Everyone was so cheerful,

loud and excited to spend time together. It was a blast seeing everyone. But, I couldn't help to want to just 'turn down the volume'. Sensory overload.

That night my brother-in-law knocked on my bedroom door to wake me up. He said his room was too cold and asked me to help him turn up the thermostat. It was set at 67. My parents lived in an old antebellum house that could certainly get chilly on winter nights. This was the warmest condition I had slept in for months though and appreciated every bit of those 67 degrees. He was unable to sleep. It was never more apparent to me just how different my brother-in-law and I viewed 'chilly'. My frame of reference for comfort had shifted dramatically.

The next day I had to catch up on Christmas shopping. With only a few days left until the holiday, the stores had been cleaned out. I had 9 nieces and nephews to consider… most under the age of 7. I went to Walmart and loaded up my cart with toys. The checkout line lasted an hour and everyone was scurrying to jump in the faster lanes. I looked at each of our shopping carts realizing how useless all of this stuff was. I mean none of us NEEDED any of it. My thru-hiking buddies had lived off of the equivalent of one of these carts for 6 months.

This reality check might be a little depressing. Calm down, you'll adjust back totally fine. I just want to mention that reentering society may take some adjusting. The positive changes drastically outweighed any of this stuff.

Personal Changes I Love.
- New Outlook on Life. I'm much less likely to get involved with something I don't want to now.

Pursuing the AT made me feel like I can reach for gold and not have to settle for anything less.

- No More Hunting. I did not grow up hunting every weekend. My dad and I would duck or turkey hunt more like a couple times a year in South Alabama. It was father-son bonding time and I enjoyed it. After the AT though, hunting lost all of its appeal. In fact, killing anything even as small as a bug has lost its appeal.
- Tougher Skin. Most hikers will talk about growing a little thicker skin after the AT. Things just don't bother you as much, especially anything related to the outdoors. Mosquitoes, cold weather, blisters, anything.
- Appreciation for Luxury. You're probably not going to complain about a tough mattress, eating bland food or a cold shower... or certainly a lot less.
- Good Friends. I still keep in touch with a lot of my hiking buddies. We had a wedding last year and all flew out to California for it.
- Badass Memories. It was a grand ole time that I look back on with fondness... and will continue to for the rest of my life.
- New Skills. I was worried about the whole job thing. On the contrary, I had a ton of ideas for a new business after the AT. I knew a heck of a lot about the outdoor industry and products on the market. I started Greenbelly Meals and have been enjoying the journey ever since. You'll have a lot of backpacking domain knowledge as well.
- New Adventures. The AT might quench your thirst for adventure or just tease your taste buds and make you even hungrier. I think, for most, it

is the latter. After the AT, I have found myself living abroad for most of the time and frequently thinking about my next new experience and challenge to pursue.

To Do After the Trail.
- Write Your Thank You Cards. I kept a list in my journal of anyone who helped me with some trail magic. It didn't come close to repaying them. But, it felt great to send out some appreciation.
- Think about getting a job in the outdoor industry. A local outfitter, an outdoor blogger, trip guide, park ranger, etc.
- Plan Your Next Hike.

My Message to You.
Enjoy it, please. It will feel like the hike is never ending… and then it will be done. There will be few experiences in your life that impact you to the degree that a thru-hike does.

Keep in touch. Safe hiking amigos,

Chris

CHAPTER 15

Wrap Up

Summary of Things to Do Now.
1) Decide if a thru-hike really interests you. List your reasons for going and for not quitting.
2) Budget it out. Give yourself a cushion and think about possibilities after finishing.
3) Pick a date to leave and which direction you want to go.
4) Take care of the home front. Bills, house, possessions, etc.
5) Get in shape (somewhat).
6) Buy gear and request sponsorships.
7) Buy plane tickets and organize logistics to the trail head.
8) Say goodbye to loved ones and take a deep breath.
9) Kick ass and take names.

Send me a picture from Katahdin.
I'd love to see your summit photo on Katahdin or Springer… or anything (fun or serious) you feel like sharing from the Trail. I might just post it on our site: chris@greenbellybar.com.

I'd LOVE Your Review.
If you found any of this book helpful, I'd love to hear your thoughts by leaving a review on Amazon. Reviews are considered to be the 'lifeblood' for books. Your review will, at minimum, help the next potential thru-hiker navigate their research process.

Resources.
- whiteblaze.net. AT hiker forum.
- trailjournals.com. Online hiking journal tool.
- appalachiantrail.org. ATC website to register.
- theatlodge.com. The trailhead hostel in Maine.
- hikerhostel.com. The trailhead hostel in Georgia.
- AWOL Guidebook.
- Thru-Hiker's Companion. Guidebook.
- guthooks.com. Guide app.

THANKS!
Thanks to everyone helped me out on the AT: Trail Angels, strangers, friends and family.

Thanks to Heather 'Anish' Anderson for the "female related" content. Keep on breaking records.

Thanks to Catherine Cage and Gordon Van Remmen.

Also, thanks to all of these people whose feedback helped contribute to this book: Adrian Gonzalez, Ampah Tivakam, Amy Walker, Andrew Baranak, B00t, Barry Tada Webb, Becca HC, Ben Baker, Ben Tarpley, Berkley Aiken, Beth W, Bill Guiffre, Billy Holley, Bill Mulvey, Blue Rudge Outdoor Exchange LLC, Bonnie, Briana, Brit Barnard, C Shireman, Caleb Aikens, Charles (EYESOLO) Graves, Christopher Freire, Christopher Loomis, Clare Pfeifer,

Clay Hildebrand aka Stuff, Contact X2445, Daniel Breskey, David Mason, Deb, Debbie Crowder aka Landcruiser, Dennis Blackerby, Diane Olans, Donald, Dos, Ebony McMurray, Elaine Holli, Ellsbug, Elwin, Eric, Eric Arthur, Fabia Liesner, Farwalker, Fireweed, Fred, Freeman, Gabbar Khai, Garth, Garth Flint, Gary Gross, Gary Kirk, Gavar Khai, Geo Goneau, Glen J. Gargano, Gordon Cherr, Gregory Caporale, Gregory Dewees, Greg Howe, Han Daddy Walsh, Harryswan Rusk, Honey Badger, J, James McGaughey, Janell Thurnauer, JC Maloney, Jeanne Schlegel, Jeff Haddix, Jeff Leagjeld, Jennifer Anderson, Jer Bear Evans, Jeremy Pruitt, Jimmy Clarke, Joanna Drzaszcz, Jodi Cox, Joe Davenport, Joel Killough, John (just John), John Zukowski, Joseph Buettner, Joseph Idell, Jukebox 500, June Quinn, Kat (Rugby), Kevin Penner, Kip, kkkkkkkk duh, Krista Vetort, Kristin Richards, Kristine Pavlik, Lance, LARRY MANZ, Larry Greer, Layne Cassidy, Lenair Ballard, Linda Visman, lois, Lt. Dennis Blackerby, Mark Coleman, Mark Schutte, Mark Whitcombe, Marvin (Bucky) Buckmaster, Mary Denison (Wenda), Melissa Katz, Merryn Coutts, Michael- Braselton GA, Michael Folmar, Michael Rittig, Mike Sullivan, Monique DiCarlo, Mont Winder, Mrs. White, Nancy Ball, Nelly Real, Nic Palmer, Pamela Roy, Pari O, Patsy Wieler, Pete Bolesh, Peter Skuse, Phil Gilbert, Pink Lady, Rachel Hopke, Ralph Calhoun, Randall Kaiser, Randy Mcintosh, Reggie, RevLee, Richard Currey, Rheta Mason, Richard Nesbitt, Rivergod, Robert MacLean, Robert Tesar, Rock Lobster, Rory Lee Russ, Sarah Dhooma, Silkstep, Snacks, Sport Jensen, Stamp Tramp, Steve, Tammy, Terence Hall, Terry Douglas, Terry Perry, The Spears, Tim Brennan, Tim C, Tiny Tim, Two packs, Vicki Gray, WC Ellett, Will Boucek, Willem, William Judd, Wunder, Yes, Yumma Aditya Prakoso.

The AT Dictionary

AMC	Appalachian Mountain Club. Organization in charge of the hut system in The Whites.
Alpine Zone	Also known as 'above the treeline'. The high-elevation areas where trees are unable to grow.
AT	Appalachian Trail
ATC	Appalachian Trail Conservancy. Non-profit organization in charge of protecting and maintaining the Trail.
Awol	'The A.T. Guide'. The only map a thru-hiker needs.
Balds	Barren areas on many mountain tops. Their existence has many theories.
Base Weight	Total Pack Weight - Consumables (food, water, etc.) = Base Weight.
Bear Bag	Hung in a tree to prevent attracting bears. Usually contains food, trash, toiletries - anything with a strong odor.
Biner	Short for 'carabiner' - the metal loop with a spring loaded opening generally used for ropes.

Bivy	Short for 'bivouac sack' - a mini tent-like shelter. Generally used in emergencies, mountaineering or ultralight backpacking.
Bladder	Or 'water reservoir'. Smaller collapsible water container.
Blaze	Used to mark the Trail. Typically a 2 x 6 inch strip of paint on a tree located about eye level.
(Aqua) Blazing	Taking a waterway instead of the Trail.
(Blue) Blaze	The blaze that leads to a water source.
(Pink) Blazing	Process of hiking with a female.
(Yellow) Blazing	Process of taking the road to the next trail head and essentially skipping a chunk of hiking.
(White) Blaze	The iconic blaze that marks the Appalachian Trail.
Bluff	Steep cliff.
Bounce Box	Box of supplies you ship or 'bounce' up to pick up in your next trail town.
Bushwhacking	Hiking off trail. Done because the trail is poorly marked, for the adventure of it or because you are lost.
Cache	A hiding place. Typically where you or a trail angel might stash food and other goodies.
Cameling Up	Drinking as much water as possible at a water source to prevent carrying it.
Cairn	A pile of rocks or stones used to mark the trail. Used in place of blazes where there are no trees.
Cathole	A hole dugout for human waste. Ideally at least 6 inches deep and at least 200 feet away from a water source.

Contour Lines	Lines used on a topographical map to display variations in elevation.
Cowboy Camping	Camping underneath the stars without a tent.
Cowboy Coffee	Mixing water with raw, unfiltered coffee grounds.
Crampons	A metal frame used on boots for traction in snowy and icy conditions.
Cuben Fiber	A high-performance fabric used as an ultralight material for some tents and bags.
DEET	Ingredient used in insect repellents - aka 'diethyltoluamide'
Double Blaze	Two blazes aligned vertically to signal a sharp turn in the Trail.
Dromedary Bag	A larger collapsible water container.
Droppin' Trou	Process of pulling down your pants (or 'trousers'). Generally shouted as a warning that you are about to change clothes.
False Summit	The sense that you are approaching the summit... and then realize it is only a small plateau teaser.
FKT	'Fastest Known Time'. The speed record held for completing the Appalachian Trail either 'supported' or 'unsupported'.
Flip-flop	Referring to the direction you are hiking. Can be thought of as hiking it in two separate 'halves' instead of one continuous stretch. Ex: ME>VA and then GA>VA or VA>GA and then ME>VA.
Footprint	A separate 'floor' of your tent used as a ground cloth or additional protective

	barrier.
Gaitors	Leggings used to protect your shins and ankles from thick brush or prevent water from draining into your feet.
Gap	The low spot on a ridge line in between mountains.
GORP	"Granola, Oats, Raisins and Peanuts" or "Good Ole Raisins and Peanuts". I just call it 'Trail Mix'.
Green Tunnel	Another term for The Appalachian Trail. Referring to the heavily wooded green forests that the Trail snakes through.
Guylines	The cord or rope used to tie down the tent or tarp.
Hiker Box	A box of freebies. Generally leftover food or gear from previous hikers often located in hostels or shelters.
Hiker Trash	A tongue-and-cheek term for thru-hikers. We have been known to resemble vagrants.
Hut	Large cabins built and maintained by the AMC located mainly in the White Mountains.
HYOH	'Hike Your Own Hike' - mentality used by thru-hikers to enjoy their time on the Trail.
Kin'lin	Small pile firewood used to ignite the fire.
Knob	Small mountain or rounded hill.
Hostel	Trail town lodging. Like a hotel room with several bunk beds.
Lean-to	A simple shelter structure comprised of a roof angled at a 45 degrees. Generally only has 3 walls.
Logbook	or 'register'. Every shelter has one. Used

	for safety to inform people of your whereabouts, communicate with other hikers, and vent about anything and everything.
NERO	A "Near Zero" day. Hiking only a mile or less.
NOBO	Northbound hiker going from Georgia to Maine.
Pocket Rocket	A Trademarked named for an MSR stove. Has become a generic term for a small fold able canister stove top.
Postholing	The process of stepping in snow and leaving a hole.
Privy	The shelter bathroom. Most of the time a simple wooden outhouse with a composting toilet.
PUDs	'Pointless Ups and Downs'. Referring to the rolling nature of the Trail.
Ridge-runner	Somewhat like an informal Park Ranger. Generally a volunteer interested in promoting respect for the Trail.
Scramble	A section of the Trail too steep or rocky to walk forcing a hands and knees 'scramble'.
Section Hiker	Someone who hikes the Appalachian Trail in sections over a longer period of time instead of a continuous thru-hike.
Shelter	Simple wooden structures scattered about every 10-20 miles along the entire Trail. Most hold around 8-12 hikers.
Slack Packing	Not carrying gear for the day. Generally this means leaving your gear in town and getting shuttled to a trailhead in the morning and picked up at a trailhead

	farther down in the afternoon.
SOBO	Southbound hiker going from Maine to Georgia.
Stealth Camping	Camping in a site that has not been used as a campsite before.
Switchback	Instead of hiking straight up a very steep incline, switchbacks are used to zigzag and lengthen the trail for a more moderate incline (or decline).
Thru Hiker	A hiker who completes the Trail in one continuous hike or within a year time frame.
Townie	'Dayhikers', 'Bathers', or people from town.
Trailhead	Where a section of trail begins. Usually at a road crossing or somewhere accessible by vehicle.
Trail Angel	A giver of Trail Magic. A volunteer who helps hikers with a place to stay in their house, a shuttle to the trailhead, free food, anything.
Trail Magic	Given by Trail Angels. The goodies a Trail Angel offers out of goodwill.
Trail Name	The name a hiker goes by on the Trail. A sort of 'alter-ego'. Almost all hikers go by a trail name.
Treeing a Bear	The act of surprising a bear and it sliding down a tree.
Triple Crown	The three major USA hiking trails: The Appalachian Trail, The Pacific Crest Trail, The Continental Divide Trail. One who completes all three is known as a 'Triple Crowner'.
UL	'Ultralight'. A minimalist and lightweight

	backpacking mentality.
Vestibule	The small 'porch' of a tent.
Widowmaker	A dead tree waiting to fall and make a widow out of the suspecting hiker's wife.
Webwalking	The process of taking the lead for the group and walking through the fresh spider webs.
Work For Stay	Instead of paying for a room, at select hostels and huts, many hikers choose to work or volunteer for a few hours.
ZERO Day	The lazy and luxurious days of hiking zero miles.

Made in the USA
Coppell, TX
08 May 2021